The Letters

Memoir of Love, Loss and Restoration

Barbara J. Spinelli

The Letters

Copyright © 2021 by Barbara J. Spinelli

All rights reserved.

Published by Red Penguin Books

Bellerose Village, New York

No part of this book may be reproduced in any form or by any electronic or mechanical means, including information storage and retrieval systems, without written permission from the author, except for the use of brief quotations in a book review.

CONTENTS

The Letters	vii
Prologue	1
Fort Jackson, SC	9
Vietnam	65
Aftermath	129
The Conversation	135
Reflections	149
Author's Note	155
Acknowledgments	159
About the Author	161
Photos	163
Reading Group Guide	171

Dedicated to all those in the circle of a loved one who has departed due to military service or any other circumstance. May you always feel the sustained presence of their eternal love.

THE LETTERS

There is a story to tell
from the yellowed pages
of many letters
neatly folded
tied with faded ribbons

Courage crouches in the corner
setting them free
places me in bondage again
if only for a while

I approach it gingerly
getting ready
straining my heart
with words deeply imbedded for
far too many years

There lies in state
a book
in a piece of vintage luggage
residing in an uninhabited space
calling my name

Coax me out on a limb
grow my wings so I can fly
with lines from my lover's pen
before the ink fades
into the darkened night

*"Life can only be understood backwards,
but it must be lived forwards."*
~Soren Kierkegaard

PROLOGUE

9/11/2020

*I*t is often said that many of our life changing experiences occurred on an average day or in an ordinary manner. This is no exception.

My life changed that afternoon. I was getting my hair colored and styled at the salon for the first time since the beginning of the COVID-19 pandemic. As I was almost finished, one of the hair stylist's husband came in speaking about the local volunteer fire department. A few words later I was in a short conversation with him about my previous connection to the fire department and mentioned one name, Lester "Chip" Cafiero.

He paused and a look of recognition crossed his brow. "I know who you are," he said. His father and Chip's father served together in the original firehouse. Back then, it was like one big family with everyone gathering together for so many events, parades and holiday celebrations. He told me about the memorial established in recent years commemorating Chip's military service. He asked if I wanted to see it. With not much time to think, and a slight hesitation, I said "Yes."

2 | THE LETTERS

Within a few minutes I was at the firehouse standing before it. Every sensation coursed through my body. As I gazed at his name and touched the miniature fire truck below the plaque, I was suddenly transported back in time. I held back my tears till I returned to my car where I wept deeply for an unaccountable amount of time.

When I returned home I went directly up into the attic to find our history which had been placed in a vintage hard shell suitcase, hidden in a crawl space and unopened for 50 years. Inside were the remnants of a life knitted together through photos, memorabilia and over 200 letters written to me throughout seven months of military service during the Vietnam War. It was like opening a time capsule. I stepped inside my past, propelling me back to 1968 with a war waging and a deep and unbounded love prevailing.

Three months later, I finished reading the letters. The grief that I thought I had securely locked away in that suitcase came roaring out. I could clearly feel his presence all around me. It's as if he wanted me to go back in time, back to him. With each letter I drew closer to him again. I could smell the intact envelopes, trace his handwriting and see more of him in the photos. It all came back to me with a rush of emotion.

He often wrote that our separation was soothed by writing to me. I understood this very well. When he died, I was in a state of shock. The only way I could find my voice was through writing. Over the years, it lifted me out of dark places.

Instinctively, I took his cue and started to write back to him in the present recalling the details of our life together, attempting to make sense of what was now happening. I felt him guiding me to the letters he would want me to choose for a reply. It became a joint project, simultaneously painful and joyful, confusing and clarifying. I didn't know it would take me on a path to breaking open and healing my caged heart.

The irony of the date of this rediscovery, the anniversary of September 11th, was not lost on me. I worked two blocks from the World Trade Center for many years, been in the towers numerous times and as so many other stories, was saved from being there because of a rescheduled meeting. Watching the second plane slice through the tower, smoke ravaging the streets, debris raining down and the loss of friends and co-workers all in small segment of time shocked me into a state of silence as it did so many years before.

Before the hair salon incident, I had watched the memorial proceedings on TV. Then, as we did every year on the anniversary, spoke with my friend and co-worker on the solemnity of the day and what we witnessed together. In some way it was like being on the front lines of a war zone together. He and I shared the harrowing memories and the anguish of the days thereafter and are somehow soothed by an unabashed check-in on our thoughts and feelings each anniversary. Then we go on with our day a little quieter but resolved to carry on. Little did I know that later in the day I would be revisiting another point in my life when nothing made sense and I would go silent once again.

THE LETTERS

. . .

March 20, 1970

Department of the Army
US Army Military Mail Terminal
San Francisco, California

The enclosed mail, addressed to Private First Class Lester V. Cafiero, Jr. bears your return address.
I regret to inform you that Private Cafiero was reported missing on 12 March 1970.
Please accept my deepest sympathy. I am truly sorry that it was not possible to have delivered this mail to him.
Sincerely,
Jose Strazzara
Acting Commander

What a hell of a job Captain Strazzara had. I imagine him typing out these letters all day and tallying the unopened mail. Possibly he had been wounded and now had a desk job. What scars did he acquire either way? He was part of that circle, like rings in a tree bark, who just slightly, but nevertheless came into the realm of a person that no longer existed. Maybe he felt something for each letter or maybe it became just part of the job. I will never know. But, there is always the writer and the receiver in correspondence. In his case, he was the middleman, transferring information from one being to another.

    He wasn't completely accurate in his details. He was reported missing in action, but he actually died on that day.

    One out of every 10 Americans who served in Vietnam was a casualty. With 2.7 million serving, and 442 casualties in the month of Chip's death alone, he was a busy fellow. That envelope had been sealed for 50 years. I gingerly opened it and discovered 17 unopened letters I had written to him. I later found out he was on a mission and wasn't getting mail for two weeks prior to his death and also the U.S. Postal Service was on strike.

We wrote daily to each other. Sometimes, we wrote several times a day. Without technology, letters were literally our lifeline. How lost he must have felt without my letters. They were probably on base waiting for him.

I carefully opened the envelope and read my unopened letters to him, finishing with my final words to him:

> "… I am so proud to be yours and have so much respect for your devotion. I know you'll always be mine and that you mean all that you say and feel. I can't wait for the day to come when I can hold you in my arms. It must come soon! Stay well. Take care of yourself. You're all mine and I'm all yours."
>
> Love, Barb

Then, I released his letters to me from the ribbon tied stacks and went back to the beginning.

"Love is a space in which all other emotions can be experienced."
~Robert Prinable

FORT JACKSON, SC

(JULY – NOVEMBER, 1969)

BEGINNINGS

Hi Love,

How is your day? You make my life so enjoyable. We share many happy moments and have a long life of love ahead of us. I enjoy sharing our love with each other and the things we do together, as one. You really showed me true happiness and most important, Barb, you showed me love.

I can remember the day we met so clearly. That day made me know what I wanted in life. The one thing neither one of us had wanted when we met was love. But, like they say, love is stronger than all of us. It just took hold of us both and pulled us together until we became one in heart and mind.

Like the night I told you I loved you. I couldn't help it. I wanted so much not to say it. I didn't want to believe I was in love. I couldn't hold back such a strong and powerful feeling. Then it turned out that you had the same feelings. I'm glad things are as they are now.

I would have searched forever for you. You're the only one I could love as I do. I never would have known love if it weren't for Gail.

Devotedly Yours,
Chip

. . .

We chose each other December 6th, 1968. I had graduated high school one year after he had, but we never crossed paths. Two years prior my family left a New York City borough and moved to our town.

In the beginning I hated living in the suburbs. I was a city gal at a young age. My family didn't have much money. They were both blue collar workers and were just getting by like so many families as part of the post WWII migration, getting a piece of the American dream by owning a home.

By age 12 I knew the NYC subway system pretty well and took three different trains each way just to get to high school. My neighborhood friends and I would take the subway into the city and hang out in Central Park. My favorite part of it was the ice skating rink in winter. We thought nothing about going down to the Village and experiencing what was then taboo. I loved the diversity, the excitement, the new experiences. I became street wise.

My parents loved the theatre, music, films and art. I was exposed to the arts at a very young age. I guess that influenced my appreciation for them and the city that housed all of that culture. Twice a year they saved up, dressed us up in our finest clothes and took us into the City for an adventure and a dinner in a nice restaurant.

But, the 60's in New York City, as with all over the country, was going through a lot of turmoil and we became more defensive. After two burglaries, a minor assault on my mother in our building (she fought the assailant off) and me escaping a scary gang on a train platform the gig was up. Off to Long Island we went.

My first several months in our town were difficult. It was one of the hottest summers on record with no air conditioning. The house needed some work and every weekend before the move was spent preparing for the move. I felt like a fish out of water.

I missed my friends. We had done everything as group of guys and gals. We sang on street corners, learned to dance with each other, roller skated everywhere, played stoop ball and learned to appreciate male and female friendships. Everyone had a similar family dynamic so we understood one another and weren't afraid to tell the truth. None of us were of driving age at the time so distance made it difficult for me to see them after we moved.

Later on when I saw the movie, Annie Hall, there was a scene where the storyteller couldn't sleep when they went out to Long Island. The crickets and birds kept him up, but not the sanitation truck noises or the ubiquitous sirens. I still laugh so hard when I see that movie. I didn't sleep for weeks and cursed those birds who woke me up at dawn! Now I feed them almost every day and welcome their morning song.

I finally assimilated about six months later, made friends and got used to a different life. One of the friends I became close with was Gail. We were polar opposites. She grew up in town and had a mother who had cocktails in the afternoon, just like on TV! Despite the different backgrounds, she took me under her wing and we formed a bond. She was tall, blond, outgoing popular, and of course had a steady boyfriend, your brother.

By our first semester in college she was obsessed with fixing me up. I wanted nothing to do with it. I had dated a bit, but no one really interested me. I was focused on college, planning my future and working.

That auspicious night she insisted I go to a party with her, figuring that she could secretly introduce us and the rest is history. I don't remember the introduction but I do remember how we started talking as if we were picking up on a past conversation, like we had known each other forever. Everything wonderful in my life came about through a twist of fate. You are at the top of the list.

You were full of life and dreams and ideas. Everything interested you. You wanted to build roads; I wanted to work in NY City in business and fly off to many destinations. As an engineering student, you were good in math and that was the one class I struggled to pass. You were training to be a volunteer fireman like your Dad. You were named after him, which is how you got your nickname, Chip.

That night, I learned you were genuine, insightful and compassionate. You wanted to know about me and listened to everything I said. I had never revealed so much about myself to anyone before.

Gail purposely left early. You took me home in that little Austin Healey Sprite as the snow started to fall. The heater in your car was temperamental but I didn't feel the cold. We talked till almost sunrise. I went home and sat on the edge of my bed and felt exhilarated and stunned, as if I was hit by a thunderbolt. I know there are lots of songs about that feeling, but for me it was new and everything changed that night. Every year since, on the first Friday of December, no matter what the circumstances, I've thought of you.

The next night we had our first date and spent a lot of time getting to know each other over the next few weeks in between school and work. You spent Christmas Eve with me and my big Italian family. You fit right in and charmed all of them. You gave me Shalimar perfume and I gave you English Leather cologne. We went to midnight Mass with the whole family. You reached out for my pinky finger and we locked hands. A few weeks later you told me you loved me and I knew I loved you. We both uttered the words we hadn't shared with anyone else before. Our fate was sealed.

That first night when we met there was a spark of passion along with a strong sense of trust. In the days and months to follow I would come to learn that my instincts about you were 100% correct. Your actions matched your words. I knew I could trust you with my heart.

HEART AND SOUL

Dear Lover,

I'm in the reception center. It's raining here now. It reminded me of walking with you in the rain, enjoying ourselves. Just like we did that time we went to the Village in New York. All I do is think of you. I miss you one hell of a lot.

Love means so much to me. I can't be without you so long. I'm hoping basic training will hurry up and get here so that I won't have time to miss you as much. I hope it works because now I think I'll go nuts if I don't see you. Time better hurry. I feel already like I'm dying without you.

You're my heart and soul. You have all my love and I want you to keep it safe. With each letter I send you, even more of my love for you is sent to keep. As fast as my love is growing, I'm sending it to you. I'm glad love is small and light or the shipping charges would cost me a fortune!

All my love,
Chip

I remember the surreal feeling when your draft number came up so low. Suddenly a war that was on the other side of the world came much closer. The possibility that our love and future could be tested became real. The newspaper articles and the television news were no longer commentaries. Our lives were becoming part of something bigger, one that was out of our control.

I now know the fragility of life and the strength of deep love. After all, even with fifty years of a full life, the wound remains. Still, I wouldn't trade any of it for all the riches in the world. What you gave me is invaluable. Reading these letters, expressions of your love and devotion, makes me grateful for the scar I carry.

With you, love was never a noun; it was always a verb. Through your words and actions, I'm beginning to allow the memories and feelings to expand my heart bathed in the knowledge of being truly loved.

BASICS

Hi Love,

I got my shots today. What a feeling. The used an air gun. It didn't hurt going in but later, Wow! They give you 8 shots with 2 guns, both at once with 4 shots in each gun. My left arm was bleeding. After about a minute it hurt a lot. I had to laugh so that I wouldn't think of it. I have to get shots once every week for 8 weeks. Pain! That's life!

We got our rifles today. Now we're killers. At least they'll make us killers pretty soon. They call us soldiers, we look like soldier and try to act like soldiers but I'll be damned if I feel like a soldier.

Tomorrow the real fun starts. I'm a little nervous, I guess. It's going to be a bad scene. I'm ready for it now. They've given us enough garbage already and I'm conditioned for it. It's like getting Novocaine for a tooth. After it wears off, it still hurts pretty bad, but not as bad as it would have without it.

I can't have soda, only milk or water with meals. I'm dying for something else to drink. I'd run 10 miles for a 6-pack of Schaefer! I'd walk 3 miles for something besides water. My throat gets dried out. I'm underfed. I eat almost anything to keep from shriveling up to nothing. I ate vegetables yesterday and an onion burger (a little chopped meat and lots of onion which they shaped into a burger). It tasted like an onion. That's G.I. life!

They say a lot of stuff about the heat and that you don't get worked too hard in real hot weather. In the last two Basic training cycles four guys died of heat exhaustion. I guess they work you hard in any weather. Tell your father I took his advice and I'm taking those salt tablets. The heat isn't getting me down. I still get tired but I think it's mostly from lack of sleep.

Tomorrow I'll be in the Army 10 days. I wish I had only days left. I'm even more yours then when I left. That's because my love grows more and more each day. I miss you very much, Love. You're the heart of my existence. Without you I'm lost. Just being away from you makes me feel terrible. You'll be getting my love with every letter I send. You deserve it. I'll be yours forever, and ever and ever......

All my love and kisses
Chip

. . .

I don't think we realize all of the conditioning we've had since we came out of the womb. Almost everything we've learned has been a product of conditioning. It starts at potty training, to school learning, inherited family scripts, work, and on and on. We get rewarded for what we do well and punished sometimes for what we don't do as well.

Your experience is a microcosm of extreme conditioning. You were being trained to live way outside of your comfort zone, to challenge yourself against measurements and to be prepared to fight and/or kill so as not to be killed. The bar is raised every day for you to advance in the achievement of goals. One needs a strong inner resolve to not lose sight of who they truly are. You were straddling two beings, the soldier and the human being. It must be difficult to fuse the two together, especially in personal relationships.

In my work I often tell clients that when we exchange a paycheck for work we are always giving up some freedom to comply with rules and regulations. There are no guarantees and freedom comes at a price.

Your ability to assess and distinguish your true feelings was an asset. Letters allow us to tell our truth to the willing recipient. You learned what you had to learn. You did what you needed to do, but your end game was always love. You chose it over bitterness. Would things have been different if we weren't in each other's lives? I'd like to think that your soul was your compass and that would have guided you either way.

SOLDIER

Hi Sweetheart,

It's me again. I got paid today; a real big $30! All together I've gotten $55 since I've been working for Uncle Sam! Today was kind of rough. At 6 a.m. I was running 150 yards with a guy on my back. Then I had to run the Run, Dodge and Jump course; then run a mile. I was tired. I did it all in about 40 minutes. We couldn't rest at all between runs. Then we had bayonet practice for an hour and then went to a marching class where we marched for almost two hours. Next I get to clean the barracks.

Next week things start getting tougher. We'll be fighting each other with giant size Q-tips. It's a combat class where you beat the hell out of each other. They give you head and groin protectors so you don't get more than a few black and blue marks. Next week things get going stronger. We have a physical training test. You have to get above 300 out of 500 to pass. It's a lot of hard stuff. I'll do my best. I think I'll do OK. If you don't pass it you have to start Basic from the beginning again. I can't do that!

While doing all that running and marching and training I

took my mind off of the heat and the hurt thinking of what you would say to comfort me, and of course, how you would kiss it all away. I love you ever so much. I'll always love you. We have a good thing going. When things are down and out, just think of the times we had together. The love we gave to each other could never be forgotten.

Whenever I have a doubt about something I just talk with you and I make it through everything just fine. It works every time. Sometimes I think I'm going nuts because I can hear you talking back and saying nice things and encouraging me to do what I'm trying to do. Then I'm not tired anymore and my muscles seem to stop hurting and I can keep on going.

I love you and cherish you and every bit of your love. Keep it up, Babe, and keep the love flowing this way. There's a river flowing from here to your house. It's overflowing. There's so much love going from me to you. Stay mine. That's an order!

All my love, kisses and devotion,
Your Chip

. . .

After reading your letters about the challenges you had in basic training, I keep thinking about that wakeup call: *Soldier, you're in the army now*! I know how tired you were on some days from training but that you also deep down liked the physicality of it. You never backed down from a challenge. That's why you loved being a fireman. When that alarm went off, you were there. I love that you had that perfect blend of purpose and fragility.

The only part of it that I can relate to was the marching part. When I was in seventh grade I became a majorette in the drum and bugle band. I learned how to twirl a baton, send it up in the air and catch it on its way down. It was great fun. The best part were the boots. They were white leather with tassels. Every step in those boots made me feel like Wonder Woman, powerful and strong, as we led the band down the neighborhood city streets.

I'm still a sucker for a great pair of boots! Of course, your marching was of a different nature.

You frequently told me that you struggled to get the right words to flow out of the pen. You thought you fell short on the ability to express your love for me. In all my years I have never known anyone who could put their feelings to words like you did. In many ways anyone who came after you couldn't reach the high bar you set. That underestimation always kept you reaching higher with a touch of innocence and wonder. I view it as your superpower.

Reality is always tougher than expected. Idealism is a luxury at times. Still, we carry on. Now I know how fragile we can be when we are broken. I know that first hand when life went on without you. I couldn't believe how much my heart actually hurt when you were gone. Not only was it an emotional pain but a physical one. I felt that part of my heart, the one connected to you, lost in the remains of you. I couldn't believe I actually stayed alive. The only way I could go on was to numb my heart. Strangely, even now, when having a physical exam I'm detached from the heart as an issue. I think that it survived because of you.

Whenever life has gotten tough and I'm hanging by my thumbs or curled up in a corner, I believe you are pulling me up as we always did for one another.

Reading your letters is repairing my heart. The feelings, tears and the pain are a reminder that I am alive and have the capacity to love with my whole being. Yours was, and mine is, a good heart.

MARRY ME

Hi, Babe

    All I ever think about is being able to be with you. We're missing so many good togetherness times. We'll just have to make them all up when I come home. You better save all your free time for me! I'm going to need it all to explain my feelings towards you. It's pure love and devotion. I want to make myself worthy of all of your love. I need your love to exist. You're my morning sunshine and the evening's beautiful sky.

    We've seen a lot of beautiful days together but nothing compares to your beauty. I love you. You are my everything. So, you better get ready to marry me, soon!! Next step is the ring, the church, the priest and Hawaii.

    If we get married when I'm on leave we could live together wherever I get stationed. If I go to Nam I get a rest & relaxation week. It's after about 4-6 months. They send you anywhere free for one week. Naturally I'd go to Hawaii and you as my wife could go there and meet me.

    If I went to Germany you could come along. There are lot of advantages. What do you think? Either way, I'm all yours and as far as I'm concerned we're married already. I really think of you as my true wife. I am too much in love for it to be any other way.

    You deserve the best of everything, but all I can give you is my best. You have it. You have everything of mine. Believe me when I say I love you more than you could ever imagine. True love is ours and needs to be protected and cherished, just like I cherish you. Be mine forever and ever. I'm yours and will be for eternity.

    Everlastingly yours,
    Chip

The first time you asked me to marry you was Wednesday, February 12th, 1969. It started snowing the Sunday before and turned into a blizzard. We had over 18 inches of snow. Back then, winters were fierce with a lot of snow. It froze so much we could ice skate on the pond in town. All the roads were closed and we couldn't get our cars out. Of course, the Austin Healey was buried for days. That was before global warming!

On Tuesday, I was in my room reading after we spoke on the phone lamenting how we couldn't see each other in person till we dug out. About an hour later the doorbell rang. It was you! You had walked about a mile and a half from the other end of town just to be with me. You said that a "little" snow wasn't going to keep us apart. I knew that day that I was loved and I wanted to spend the rest of life with you.

My parents said you were crazy with your nose all red with frost. I caught their smiles because they also had already fallen in love with you. My Dad lived to 97 and I never saw him light up with any other man in my life after you.

The next day we were off from classes for Lincoln's birthday. We spent the day together and with the sun bouncing off the snow you told me how much you loved me and asked me if I would consider marrying you when we graduated from college. My heart was pounding and I had tears in my eyes when I said "yes." Your beautiful blue eyes twinkled with relief and happiness.

Three months later we were in New York City at a Youth Fair. The admission price was $2.50 and in addition to films, art and photo exhibitions there was music. Some of the headliners were Tommy James and the Shondells, Jay and the Americans, and Brooklyn Bridge. There were vendors selling all kinds of trinkets, clothes and fun jewelry. You asked me to pick out a ring. I chose the one with the clear shank and two purple Lucite "stones." You asked me again if I was serious when I said I would marry you and I said *"of course,"* as if fate already sealed the deal. You placed it on my ring finger, smiled at the vendor and said, *"I'm the luckiest guy in the world."* I still have that ring!

Later on that day, we took a walk in Central Park and you

spoke to a police officer and told him we just got engaged and was going to marry. The police officer was so nice. He said he would marry us. I don't know how you got him to do it but he did. We said our vows to each other and then he said, "By the power vested in me by the City of New York, I now pronounce you man and wife!" We sealed it with a kiss. I remember the police officer's round, smiling face. I think we were the highlight of this day. There wasn't a license but from that moment on, we considered ourselves married and committed to each other for life.

We loved the City even during its gritty times. We enjoyed art, films, nature and especially music. You always made everything a lot of fun. We were never bored. We didn't have enough time to do everything we wanted to do. I'm glad I kept a calendar chronicling our time together. It is filled with memorable moments and adventures. It was also locked away with the letters.

We knew we needed to wait to formally marry. We really wanted to have our education behind us. We were committed to each other but still had our individual aspirations which we never denied each other. That's why I didn't feel like I was losing anything by marrying you. I felt I found a part of me that didn't exist before you. The times spent with you together and apart are still the most treasured memories I have.

When you were drafted and went away our separation brought us so much closer. We could speak once a week when you were in the States. But, the daily letters back and forth were the glue that held us together. With every letter, I grew closer to you in every aspect of a relationship.

It may have seemed abrupt to the outside world, but time took on a different meaning for us. We both had made decisions after carefully weighing the details of a situation and applied common sense. I felt comfortable knowing that we also were insightful and we didn't take anything for granted. Of all your qualities, your sense of integrity and generous spirit, were the most admirable. Many times you would stop to help a stranger to fix a tire or pay for the toll for the car behind us.

I had deep wounds from your death, but I was never hurt by you. We looked out for each other's interests and we protected what we had together. To marry you was the easiest decision I ever made.

BIRTHDAY

Happy Birthday, Baby,

Today I owe my thanks to your Mom and Dad for bringing you, my darling, into this world for me. You were meant for me and I for you for 18 years today. For so long, Love, we went without each other. I, wandering around without giving or receiving love for my first 18 years and 9 months of my life, finally stumbling blindly into a world of beauty and happiness. For nine months now I've been in a totally new state of mind. Now, for the first time in my life, everything I do has a meaning for <u>us.</u> Now we think, live, enjoy and love as a team; an indestructible team of eternal love and devotion.

My Love, you're the loveliest person on earth. My love and life is yours. I live only for you and your happiness. To please you is to please myself. Birthdays are a happy occasion, but today it is a very sad moment in my life. Kisses will be coming from everyone but not from me today. I, the one who adores your every movement, will be forced to wait for my kiss. It's a heartbreaking experience to face.

Have a very, very happy birthday. Today is your day. Try to think of me today while you are doing whatever you're going to do. You have all my love, honor, devotion and trust.

All my life and love,
Chip

When I think of all of the beautiful cards I've received over the years, this heartfelt birthday letter remains the best. I felt the same way when I couldn't be with you for your birthday. You were already in Vietnam for two months.

We give so much energy to a day or a holiday. What I learned from these months of spending a lot of time by myself is that we can make a celebration any day for the smallest of things. I no longer wait for a special occasion to open a nice bottle of wine or eat a delicious meal.

You made so many ordinary days special for me. I've had a lifetime of birthdays from those memories. I wasn't shortchanged. I gained appreciation for the simple things in life. We always did our best for each other. This letter will be read every year on my birthday as long as I am alive.

THE VOW

Hi Babe,
*   Here's a poem I really like. It came from a book of poems on love and marriage:*

What is Love?
To love very much is to love inadequately; we love—that's all. Love cannot be modified without being nullified. Love is a short word but it contains everything. Love means the body, the soul, the life, the entire being. We feel love as we feel the warmth of our blood, we breathe love as we breathe the air, we hold it in ourselves as we hold our thoughts. Nothing more exists for us. Love is not a word; it is a wordless state indicated by four letters.
*   ~ Guy de Maupassant*

I dreamt of being with you last night. I hope the time goes by fast so it will be more than just dreams of togetherness. I feel so empty without your presence. I'm filled with love and there is no way to let my love escape to you. My letters always contain my love but I want to be able to tell you while we're sitting close and I'm kissing your tender lips. You can't know my feelings or believe them until I can tell you of them. In writing they seem small because of a lack of words to explain them. To describe my feelings, we must be close. Then, you'll find out how very much I love you.

It's such a powerful love and so meaningful. No one else could ever make me feel like you do. You're so kind and thoughtful, mature and sexy and I could go on forever for you're the greatest; the best of everything put into one special woman, and you're mine to devote my life and my love to. I consider our love as being married. Our love is sincere, strong, dedicated, and everything that love is in a strong marriage. The only difference is the piece of paper and the walk down the aisle. That is something we'll have to work on.

I love you Barb. You are the answer to all of my dreams of love. They all came true when I met you. Now we're together in our own world of love. We're here to stay, in love forever, better or worse, sickness and health, and all the rest.

We're married! I just like to say it. I'll give you a written guarantee that I'll be yours. Write or type it up if you want. I'll sign it. Make a copy for each of us. You sign yours; I'll sign mine.

Eternally yours,
Chip

The Vow
I am yours now and forever and always will be.
I'll be with you always. When I come home we will never be apart.
I will always love you, comfort you, honor and cherish you and forsake all others,
keeping you only for me and I only for you,
as long as I shall live.

With Everlasting Love & Devotion

Forever Yours,
Your husband,
Chip

I signed and sent mine to you. You returned this one to me. We kept it with us in a safe place close to our hearts. This is the second time we formalized our commitment to each other. It was understood with our families and friends that we were united. The formalities would have to wait. The poem said it all.

Marriage was the furthest from my mind before I met you. I wasn't your typical gal waiting for Prince Charming to walk down an aisle and make my life worthwhile. I merely glossed over fairy tales as a kid. Other aspirations enticed me.

There was a whole world out there and I wanted a piece of it. I wasn't thinking about the usual futures for girls in the 1950's. I saw myself in a suit, going to meetings, making decisions. I dreamt of conference rooms instead of living rooms. Marriage seemed to be stifling and a boundary I didn't need. I had enough of those in family, church and school rules.

Sitting in third grade gazing out the school window I

watched for incoming planes headed for the airport. I would see them and whisper to myself the name of the air carrier, daydreaming about the places they had come from and where they would be going.

You came along and I didn't have to give up on those things. We carved out a niche to include our dreams into our love. I knew enough at that time there would be compromises but I was willing to let love grow and see where it took me, with or without a plane ride.

I'll never know how things would have turned out if you had returned intact and we followed our plans. Would the war have changed you? Would you have physical and emotional scars? Would my expectations have changed? These questions have entered my mind from time to time over the years, particularly over the issue of building a family together. Revelations from these letters assure me that we would have worked through it all together.

I've had a very interesting life so far with few regrets. I've travelled quite a bit, spend a lot of time in business and conference rooms, negotiated deals, reinvented myself several times, took flying lessons and had many other memorable experiences. I've never exhausted my love for flight. But, my heart has never soared like it did with you. I never felt suffocated by you. You also had the need for the balance of intimacy and freedom. You left room for both of us to grow.

After you, I have not been without love but they have never had the dimension that you provided. When you departed, my relationship instincts became cautious and erratic. Perhaps, it has been you all along that has navigated me through this quagmire. You are helping me to repair these injuries, reminding me what real love sounds and feels like. I trust you again to guide me forward.

SLEEPLESS

Hi Again Love,
  I'm on guard duty now. I was supposed to go on a 2 hr on, 4hr off shift. Instead I volunteered for a 2 on, 2 off shift. It means less time for myself, but I'm out at the landmine range. I don't have to walk around. I sit here all night. The bad part is that I have to stay here for the full time. I can't leave when I have my 2 hours off. That means I have to sleep out here. It's in the middle of the woods and thy left me without a light or my weapon. I have a stick in case I find a snake around.
  Last night I got 5 ½ hours sleep. That's about average here. I'm getting used to it. I can make it through the day but I have trouble in lectures. I fall asleep and get woken with a bang on the head. I try to learn all I can. I take most of my training seriously and think about what is being said. I figure if I learn it now maybe it will be useful sometime.
  Most of this stuff is done differently in combat. They show the correct way. In combat it's done in a cross between correctly and most rapid way. It's up to the individual to make the choice. They try to tell you how this training make you "combat ready." They build up your confidence. In basic they tell you're all going to die. Then, they say we're all going to live and no one will die. They go from one extreme to another.
  This week we start our fire training on the M-60 machine gun, the rifle grenade, the rocket launcher and the 50 caliber machine gun. It'll be an interesting week but bad for our free time. Every time we fire these weapons we have to clean them. It's normal to clean from 7:00 p.m. to 1:00 a.m. after firing. They're very strict about cleaning the weapons. A dirty weapon means an Article 15 automatically.
  It's a lucky thing I called last night. If I didn't you wouldn't have heard from me. I would have never been able to call tonight. Talking to you last night made today seem like Monday. I always feel so much better after talking to you. Just your voice soothes me.

I always forget all my headaches from the week. It helps a lot because then I start the week off with a clear mind and no bad thoughts about anyone.

By the end of the week everyone is turning on one another. Pressure builds up inside and a lot of guys explode. Two more guys went AWOL yesterday. Everyone is talking about the guys who left. There are about 15 AWOL's already. It's a lot of work here and a lot of self control. It can really mess up a guy's mind. By Friday I'm all jumbled up and touchy. To top it off, the sleep factor wrecks the morale of everyone.

It's beautiful here. The sky is a light blue and all the pines stand tall blending with the sky. It looks like a picture. You would really like this place for a vacation. I would if it wasn't for this Army. Without your love I'd be dead. I miss you so much. I live to hold you always near me. You are beautiful in every way, even when you drop cream covers in my coffee!

There is so much about you that makes me want to love you. I could name so many things. The one big thing is that you love only what you want to love. You're truthful about your feelings of love. I know you love me and I feel so confident in your love. I realize that you're mine forever, as I am yours. We both want that and are both willing to work for it.

All My Love
Your Husband, Chip

I loved that you shared the details of your daily life there as I shared mine with you. I think a life together is made up of so many small details that get blurred over time. Through the letters we were speaking to each other about those details that we didn't want to waste time on during our brief Sunday night phone calls.

Some of the details are so clear. Remember when you asked me to go with you to pick out some new clothes? It seemed so ordinary, yet you wanted my opinion because you wanted to look nice when we went out together. We laughed a lot with you going in and out of the dressing room showing me the pants and shirts you chose. You didn't need me to go with you that day. You had been dressing yourself pretty well up till then, but you wanted to share that ordinary excursion with me and we laughed about the "fashion show" till our bellies ached afterwards. It's those small, everyday moments that make me glad I chose you and you chose me.

The thing I really appreciated about you is that you were a guy who wanted to talk out any disagreements we had before they festered into grievances. I'm not sure where you learned that, perhaps you had that example from your parents. You were wise beyond your years about that. You didn't have a thirst for hiding behind your thoughts. We knew every moment was precious, particularly when you were drafted, and we agreed not to waste it on unspoken annoyances. I found that so refreshing. In other aspects of my life I had to please everyone. With you, it pleased me to tell the truth. You accepted it willingly.

SMOKY

Hi Babe,

Come hold my hand. I feel so damned lousy. Today was the most terrible day I've had in many years. What a combination of events.

It started this morning. Some dumbbell stole a 45 caliber pistol. Since 12 p.m. (when they found it was missing) until 10 p.m. tonight we have been worked to death. I never stood at attention for such a long period of time. They wrecked the inside of my locker in a shakedown inspection looking for it. It's still missing so they confined us to the barracks for the weekend. Nice, huh?

Then came good old mail call. What I needed was a letter from you. Well, as fate had it, I didn't get one. That made two days straight and I felt low. I got a letter from home. It was all about what's new in the fire department and the home front. Pa told me how Smoky went running into the woods and went for a swim in the reservoir. Then he came to the next part. Smoky is dead. He started having trouble with his bladder. Ma and Pa took him to the Vet and they said they couldn't help him. It's a long and very sad story. The only way to help him was to put him to sleep. Now he's gone.

I still find it hard to believe. I had to read the letter about six times before I got to the end. It's funny because I read all the way to the part about Smoky and then we went to eat. While I was on line for food I decided to read some more. I had to smile and let out a few chuckles about his run in the woods. I pictured all the times I was with him and he did the same thing. Then the smile turned to tears. I just left and walked around thinking. I felt like just sitting down and crying. The tears were already in my eyes. Every time I tried to finish the letter they came back.

You wouldn't believe how close I felt to Smoky. He was just that king of guy. You'll probably feel funny when you read this. You knew him too. Right now I need you desperately. Only you could lift up my spirits. I know if we were together, I wouldn't feel so bad. I must go now. I'll write more tomorrow.

I love you,
Me

. . .

I remember when Smoky died. Your parents couldn't speak to anyone about it. I'll never forget how many times we laughed around him. He was a Dalmatian with a unique personality. You got him from a member of the fire department. He enjoyed being the mascot and loved the fire trucks. At first, he was a little jealous of me being around you; but he came around.

You learn a lot about a person watching them interact with children, animals and people in general. They were drawn to you as I was. Underneath the manhood was a child at heart with a large capacity for love that transcended age, species and environment. You could be insightful one minute and silly the next. You would have made a great father and I'm sure our home would have been filled with pets.

I know the bond between humans and an animal. My dog is going into his 11th year. He's my buddy. We take long walks together and have a lot of fun. He's still learning new tricks. Sometimes I think he understands what I'm saying to him. Mostly, he has selective listening, usually when it involves treats.

I read somewhere that when we bring a pet into our lives we must prepare to most likely outlive them. I don't think it's possible to prepare for the separation. They become a part of our lives and our story. They have a place in our hearts as do humans.

I was touched by your tears in the midst of the environment you were in. Isn't that so much like the experience of life? One minute we are laughing, and the next crying. It's what makes us human. It means we have a capacity for love. And you, darling, certainly had volumes of love to share.

I was near the reservoir today. Since last year I've been walking in the park and around the lake almost every week. I've been strangely drawn back to the park even before this rediscovery started. I have fond memories of us in the park together.

One day I went searching for that tree with our initials on it. I realized how ridiculous that was. First, there must be thousands of trees in that park. Secondly, I looked up and saw how tall those trees are and by my estimation if the average tree can grow almost two feet a year, those initials are way up near the heavens. Good Lord! Even a feisty squirrel couldn't find them. But, they are there somewhere in the park we shared so many years ago. That's good enough for me.

SOUNDS

Hi Love,

This has been a tough day. After marching for two hours we learned how to handle M-67 hand grenades. They are exactly what are used in Vietnam. Man, they are powerful and terribly loud! We also had to throw dead ones and go through simulated courses. There was a lot of crawling and running. On top of that, it rained heavily. We ran, sat, crawled and rolled in mud and water all day.

Tomorrow we start Intensive Individual Training. We crawl under barbed wire and over walls and logs all day. At night we do the same course except they shoot

M-50 machine guns at us (live rounds three feet above the ground) and there are explosive booby traps and lightly explosive charged land mines. If a mine goes off or booby trap rocks fly around, we get black and blue.

Enough about my worries. I made it this far, so I'm sure I can take another two weeks of it. Your love will help me through the days. Your love is so strong that I can feel it all the time. Without that I would be going crazy! It's so strong and growing constantly.

Babe, I'll always be yours. There isn't any doubt about that. I could never leave you. We will never part. Our love is much too strong to ever be broken. Good attitudes, hard work, confidence, trust and prayers will keep us going stronger and stronger forever. We have all that it takes. I love you beyond belief. I trust you and your good judgment under any circumstance. I want to be worthy of your loving devotion. All of my decisions are made for us, not for me.

You brought a whole new world to me, a world of love. I never knew that two people could ever feel so much for each other. You make my life so wonderful. Even being apart, you still make everything so much better. I always hear your voice saying "I love you." I am never apart from your love.

I love you, Darling,
Your Chip

When one discovers they are truly loved it changes everything. Rockets can be going off (and they were), but there is a calmness deep inside when you know you can trust another human being to have your back. There's a sense of completeness between two souls.

I've been sure of some things in my life, but never as much as I was about your love for me. You kept your word and risked rebuff to express your feelings. How could I not feel safe bathed in your loving arms and words.

You stirred something inside of me that burst open my heart. It still does. No matter how fierce or loud that ammunition was, my heart grew much stronger and bolder for you. Even though the sounds of that war are now quiet, you left me with a legacy of a deep and abiding love.

In the stillness of the night, I too, can sometimes hear your voice saying "I love you" and I know that in the end, everything will be alright.

SOUVENIERS

Hi Babe,

News of today—we are the only couple still hanging in there. The rest of my friends here have all lost or gave up their girls. Today two guys broke up their relations. One guy was caught going home for a weekend and going to another girl instead of his own. She found out he was home and never looked her up to tell her. Nice guy, Huh? The other just fought over the phone and hung up on her. The rest lost their girls to other guys and one girl decided to break her engagement because she "lost her love" for him a week after they spent a weekend together.

Everyone is still surprised we're still going so strong. I try to explain that it's because of our "love", not the stuff they call love. Someday they'll learn all about it. I never knew love until I met you, but it's real easy to know that it's love and not a fling. I feel good that you're still hanging in and waiting so patiently. When I come home, I'll try to make up for all of the time we've been apart.

I'm going to enclose one of my dog tags for a little souvenir. I don't know what you can use it for, maybe a key chain. It's been a part of me since I left so I figure I'll share it with you. Now you have one of the originals and I have one. I have to get one to replace the one I send. I must have two on me at all times. They send them home if you die in combat.

Love,
Chip

. . .

The dog tag was not in the suitcase. I don't know what happened to it. Why do we need objects to remind ourselves of the other? To your point, I suppose it's because we want to feel closer to the person when apart.

Here's what I did find:

Pressed flowers from a corsage with pink and blue ribbons and the pearl head stickpin for a dinner/dance we attended. I remember how you blushed when you pinned it on the strap of my aqua dress before we left. I swear there's a faint scent of that rose!

Various cards for different occasions including a huge 15" x 8" *Missing You* card. I have no idea what postage was needed to send that!

Restaurant menu's from our New York City escapades, newspaper clippings from events we attended, a stirrer and matches from the Copacabana, movie stubs, a "smile" button, a napkin signed by both of us "*Barbara & Chip were here-1/22/69*", various photos, a tape you made, a lock of your hair, the ring you bought me in New York City, a Sweetheart pin and a satin wall hanging from Fort Jackson that says:

SWEETHEART - I LOVE YOU
I thought that you
would like to know
That someone's thoughts
go where you go.
That someone never
can forget
The hours we spend
Since first we met,
That life is richer,
sweeter far,
For such a sweetheart
as you are.
And now my constant
prayer will be,
That God may keep
you safe for me.

Ok, I admit it's a little corny, but how I relish every remnant of you. When someone we love is gone everything left behind takes on a new meaning. There's an association more than tactile or visual. It's the remembrance of building a life together. These items are the part of the brick and mortar that builds the foundation for a lifetime of memories.

All this time they were concealed, set aside, too painful to touch, smell or feel. Now they are a salving balm, a healing reminder of love in its first bloom, untethered by circumstances of age, change and decisions made. They are symbols of love in its purest form.

I am re-experiencing it again. Some days, I feel that I'm that younger self, so assured of my footing from being loved. The proof exists. I am touching each item as if I was unpacking a priceless antique. Time has not weakened any of it; instead, it has brought me fully present in the past. Time is no longer linear; it floats back and forth. I straddle two worlds, more deftly now, as I explore your words and ignite my memories. You are my lantern in the dark.

PAIN

Hi Love,

The day's finally through. It was a long one. We double timed about one mile and marched the other 1 ½ miles to the rifle range this morning. We stayed there from 8:00 a.m. until 4:30 pm.

They're working us harder and harder each day. I'll give it a real hard rating but not a bad one. It's hard to explain. When they make me do things, I feel like I'm about to fall, but it's surprising how much pain and strain the body really can take. I handled everything they had for me so far. I really don't know how, and believe me it hurt a lot, but for some reason (YOU), I kept pushing on and made it.

When I come home you better save all your free time for me. I'm going to need it all to explain my feelings towards you. My heart is pure only for you. I want to make myself worthy of all your love. You're my morning sunshine and the evening's beautiful sky. For me, you are my everything.

We fit so well together. Do you think the same? I always do. It's the greatest feeling.

It's that time again. Lights out!

I love you,
Chip

. . .

I understand about pushing through the pain. For me, it's more about the emotional pain. I find it easier to work through the physical painful moments maybe because I know there's a beginning and an end.

The psyche is different because it's multidimensional. Many times, I don't feel the emotional pain till much later and then it's more difficult to identify its origin and even then it can't be fixed with an analgesic. To your point, knowing you are supported and loved can make a difference, but not always. I've learned that we can love another person with the deepest emotions but we can't fix what ails them. That's their journey and not ours to take on.

Our country was also in pain at this time. This was the summer of 1969. The streets were filled with anti-war protests and unrest. The war was deeply polarizing. We talked about it quite a bit. You were ambivalent. I, on the other hand, hated the war.

I remember sitting on campus and watching the protesters. I wanted to get up and scream my head off with them - "Stop the war!" "Bring our soldiers home!" But something prevented me from doing it. I think my father wrote to you, 'love the soldier; hate the war.' I was conflicted. I supported you all the way but I felt helpless in defending why we were there. I retreated, keeping my thoughts to myself. I needed to be there for you. I was in a love bubble that wouldn't allow for dissent. I don't think I had the wherewithal at that time to balance the two.

On the other hand, two other events were very exciting during the summer of '69. On July 20th Apollo 11 successfully landed on the moon. When Neil Armstrong emerged and walked on the moon, I was completely mesmerized. Outer space seemed so much closer that day. There was a world outside of what was happening here on earth. Whenever I'm in a plane I go into the deepest of sleep with absolutely no fear. I feel safer in flight than on the ground.

Many years later I became a docent at the Cradle of Aviation Museum which now sits on the same campus I attended at that time. I learned so much from the retired pilots and men who worked on the lunar module. I would listen to their stories and imagine myself in their place.

If it was a different time and circumstances I would have loved to be in space or fly jet fighters. Amelia Earhart remains one of my heroes. I've read as much as I could about her and her last flight. Whenever I cross the Pacific I look down wondering where the remnants of that flight remain.

The other exciting event was Woodstock. If you were home I bet we would have driven up there. All the musicians we loved were there. We probably wouldn't have gotten through the traffic and maybe turned off by the drugs, but what an experience it would have been! I had the opportunity to go with friends but turned it down to go to work. Duty called! They came back with some interesting stories. I guess I wasn't sure enough of myself to tempt fate.

One of the paradoxes in life is that even though we are feeling pain, life goes on around us and we can experience magic if we are open to it. And, yes, I did feel the same and it was a great feeling. I can attest to the fact that love and pain can coexist side by side. No regrets.

DETAILS

Good Morning Love,

How are you today? I wish we could spend today together. We always spent Sundays together. Those days were always happy ones. Maybe you feel the same way. I really miss those days. They were all ours. We had so many good times.

There are many more to come. I can't wait till 4:30 so I can call you. I want to hear your voice. It's so reassuring when I hear you. It makes things seem to be easier. After talking to you, the week seems to go faster. You always have those right words that ease the tension.

I think a lot about our future. In fact, I dream a lot of it. I want to spend my life working for you and giving my love to you. You mean everything to me. I feel so good when I please you and make you happy. I really enjoy doing things for you. I like when you come to me for help. I want to give of myself to you. That makes me happy-to help you when you are in need. I'm always willing to help you out in anything.

I felt good that day when you had the car accident at college and you called me. Remember, call or ask if ever you're in a jam; I'd like to help your Ma and Pa too. Tell them I'm always willing to lend a hand if needed. After all, we're all one big family now.

I love you Barb. I want to be with you now. I want to hold you close and feel your face and neck with my hand and touch your lips. I'd like to rub your warm back and feel my hands on your flesh. Your skin is so soft and smooth. I want to kiss you and hold you tight. It won't be long now and all the wants will be satisfied. I can't wait for that first kiss when you meet me at the airport!

I'm going to say good bye for now. Keep my love a part of your every day.

Love forever,
Chip

. . .

So much of life is unseen. We pass thousands, perhaps millions, of people in our lifetime. We miss the passing clouds and abundant stars and most of what others say. When we stand still and open ourselves to life and love the payoff is invaluable. So much of life is made up of a galaxy of details, moving from one task to another, bypassing the good stuff.

You paid attention to those details. You recognized the subtlety in human nature and me. All pretenses melt away and we are free to be ourselves. No guardrails are needed. We are as close to our authentic selves. What a privilege to have been seen and known by you.

When I pay attention to your words and the feelings they evoke everything seems clearer and brighter. There were so many details that passed between us; enough to last a lifetime.

I am keenly aware of the memory of my hands running through your reddish tinged hair, the sparkle in your eyes, the curl of your lips, the touch of your hands, the strength in your arms and legs, the comfort of your shoulder and the outline of your chest. I can still capture the feeling of how your body responded to me and I to you. Our bodies came together so easily.

Some nights when I'm drifting off to sleep I can still remember the sound of your voice, and the scent of your skin as I trace my hands over your body ever so slowly and feel you pulse through me. On those nights I am certain that death didn't have the power to part us.

CHALLENGES

Hi Love,

It's getting closer and closer to the end now, Love. Pretty soon we'll be together. I can't wait! Our hearts will be so close. Yep, soon bad times will turn to good times. Long awaited moments will come true.

Today is 100 days apart and 100 days I've been waiting for a kiss and a hug. I love you so much but I can't do anything but tell you so. It's a hard thing to be separated from someone you love. We both learned that. There's nothing we can do now but bear with all the pain and hope times goes by fast. Just remember that after it's over things will be smoother and our love will be stronger. Everything will become what it was before we parted.

You have it hard. I'm glad you don't let it get you down. Whenever I think I have it bad, I just think of how you must feel. You have a lot of freedom to make choices. Whenever you go someplace, you must have a lot of chances to try another love. It's up to you to weigh the facts and decide. I'm glad you are a very mature woman. I don't worry about that because you have my trust in you. I really feel good that we have trust in each other.

Take care. Stay mine. I'll be seeing you soon.

Love,

Chip

· · ·

I am so glad that you acknowledged the struggles of the people back home who love you. Too often we neglect to notice how a deployment or any lengthy separation places challenges on a relationship and a family. The issues we face go beyond the question of faithfulness, although assurances are fortifying on either end.

A bigger challenge is being the custodian of the relationship without the immediacy of sharing the ordinary occurrences and needs of the day. We are a team, yet our partner isn't near. There are decisions to be made; actions to be taken. The physical comfort of an embrace is elusive. In today's world of technology where we can see and hear each other, still, the lack of physicality creates a void.

We also live with a heightened sense of alert of what can happen, making it more difficult to live in the moment. There is a precarious emotional component at times that can usher in demoralizing thoughts, wreaking havoc on an otherwise optimistic outlook.

I felt close to you from holding up from my end. Besides letters, I was happy to send packages of your favorite food, photos, books, jokes and enjoyed us working on a crossword puzzle together, eventually finishing it together. It made me happy to return the comfort and joy you gave me. I knew that anything from home brought you closer to me.

I was ok with missing the birthdays, anniversaries and holidays together but it was a struggle to fit in when many of our friends were here and together. It's amazing how life goes on around us. All those everyday things we take for granted are still there; but, you are not.

We hide our fears so as not to shake the other or the foundation of the relationship. We gladly hold up both ends with our love, but it isn't easy. We are keenly aware there is so much that is uncontrollable. The military is making the decisions and we don't have a say in what is dictated about your next move which consequently affects us both.

By you recognizing both sides of the equation, it gave me great strength. Fidelity was never an issue for me. It was what the separation and war would do to us, together and as individuals. Could there be emotional wounds I could not heal? Would we have enough to underpin what we had with the gravest of outcomes? I didn't know at the time that it would take all of the courage and strength I could muster to deal with the gravity of permanent separation without your earthly presence.

ORDERS

Hi Love,

Well, no more Basic Training!! Graduation is over. Things are getting better now. It means that it won't be long until I'm home with you again. The half way mark is here. Thanksgiving Day should start my 30-day leave. It sounds so far away but really it's not.

I felt so bad when I told you on the phone about my orders and you cried. I wasn't going to say anything until I got home, but

I figured it would be best to tell the truth. I guess there's nothing I could do to break the news easily. I was ready for it, so when I heard it, it didn't bother me. I'm not worried about going. I know I will be scared when I leave from California. I knew it would be like that. I'm ready for anything, except losing you. That will never happen, so nothing will be getting me down.

It's too early to get that let down. Don't forget the maximum time we'll be apart now is 18 weeks: 8 weeks Basic, 2 weeks Leadership and 8 weeks AIT (Advanced Infantry Training). After that I'll be home for 30 days. Remember that after 30 days I go to California and I get my jungle fatigues, shots and an M-16. After 2 days in California I go halfway around the world. There I stay for 60 weeks. Now, that's a long time being apart. Think about that.

I'm happy it's only 10 weeks. It's long enough, but at least now I know I will get home to you. Next time I'll have a lot more to worry about. See, things aren't too bad yet.

Everything that I do is always for you. Your breath is mine. Your heart beats for me and mine for you. Things are going to work out for us. A love like ours can take care of any obstacles which get in our way. Our love can make it through it.

Love and Total Devotion to You
Chip

. . .

I have the same gut wrenching reaction now to your orders as I did back then. The truth hurt but had to be told. We were honest with each other and I believe I always knew, as you did, that you would be going to Vietnam. I held out for hope that things would be different but the reality of war was greater. The escalation statistics were not in our favor. We had to face that, as we did everything else.

All through Basic Training you did well. Receiving that expert marksmanship medal didn't help things. Or maybe, it was just a numbers game and you got the short straw. Isn't it interesting that the things we are so good at could get us into difficult situations.

You always seemed to look on the bright side of things. I'm more pragmatic than a full optimist. I hope for the best and plan for the worst. After the realization I decided to be strong for you and look forward to the limited time we would have together. You would need me to be your steady rock. I would falter at times, but I knew I would do whatever was needed for us and our future. Truth was a bitter pill I could swallow. You would do the same if the tables were turned. I would not retreat. I was all in.

DISAPPOINTMENT

Hi Love,

I went to the airport tonight with intentions of coming home for the weekend before I start AIT training. Instead, here I am now sitting in the barracks. No flights. The flight I was going to come home on was grounded in New York because of mechanical difficulties. I could have been home to you by this time. They said if I stayed at the airport until 1 a.m. I MIGHT be able to catch a flight. The one I had was switched to another flight but then both flights were full to capacity. It wouldn't have worked to be back by Sunday night if I waited for the next morning's flight with no guarantees for a flight home Sunday. I would have had only one night home.

I'm so damn mad that I'm stuck here. I wouldn't mind it so much, but now I have to wait till November to see you. I wish here and there were the same place. I want so very much to be near you. When I got to the airport I felt so good because I imagined I'd be near you soon. Oh, to be with you again!!

You give me so much love. We belong to each other. No want could ever make me turn to anyone but you. No one can compare in love or beauty with you, Darling. I'm so lucky to have you for my very own. Someday soon the aisle will be ours and the altar will be filled with the love of marriage. That day will be the best day in both of our lives.

I love you. You know how much those three words mean to me. They cannot fully explain the feeling. They would mean nothing if they were said to anyone else. Only lovers as we could understand the deepest thoughts and meaning of that one phrase. Many precious moments are set into those words.

Our love is here to stay, Babe. Never forget my love for you. Never give up hope. I love you and I will for eternity. Once again, I will sign off with all my love and devotion.

Love & Kisses
Chip

. . .

Don't you hate it when you have something fun or important planned and the weather or airlines don't cooperate? I once almost missed the appointment for the submission of my thesis to complete my Masters Degree. I got to the airport and all flights were suspended due to adverse weather conditions until the next morning. A last minute work meeting had me traveling to North Carolina. I was determined to make that deadline. I stayed at the airport till I could get the first flight early the next morning to make the deadline. The ground crew was *ALMOST* sure I could get on it.

When I finally got home I raced to the campus to keep my appointment and got it in on time. I guess it's all about timing and, of course, weather, neither of which we can control. Oh, but how frustrating!

We were both so disappointed that we had to wait two more months to see each other. You did get a reprieve when I received this letter capturing the essence of your love for me. Almost all of your letters are filled with these sentiments, even in between your grueling training schedule. Many of those letters are quite intimate and beautifully written, recalling the details of our special times together. Those letters are only for our consumption. Is that you grinning back at me?

NOSTALGIA

Hi Love,

I've moved into new barracks. They have air conditioning, thick beds and only 10 guys to a room. I'm finished unpacking. I marked up my clothing. It's very hectic now. There's an inspection in a little while.

Your picture is here to keep me going. I got it on a shelf in back of my bunk. Now I can look at it all the time. I like to lie on my bunk and just look and hope. I guess it will never happen, but I'm waiting for the day it comes alive and lays down next to me. I have to wait 62 days for that to happen. I'll be waiting.

It was real good talking to you tonight. I felt so bad when I came out of the movie. I had to call you from the first phone I saw. It was a good movie but it made me miss you so very much. They had a part in Central Park right by the lake. It was so much like the day we were there. We sat and talked on the hill. Remember? They showed a couple walking down a street. We walked a lot like them, together hand in hand.

I had to hear your voice. Just hearing you is so reassuring. All I want is to be with you for the rest of my life. I can't wait until that day comes. I love you so very much. I'm all yours.

Whatever I give to you, I receive from you to take its place. There are never any empty moments in my heart or mind. It's a special relationship that we have. It's a super love with all the extras! Nothing could break us apart. The love between us is too strong. You're mine and I'm lucky that I'm yours.

Keep up your school work and don't let things get you down. I'm backing you 100%. You better do well. I'll give you 100 kisses *for every 0.1 point over 2.8 average and 50 for 0.05. Deal? We sure are going to have a lot of kisses to pay each other. Our lips will be stuck together. That will be fun. We could hold the record for the longest kiss. We already have the greatest love award!*

I feel like writing all night to you about my love for you and the relationship we share, but I must go now. Lights out in 5 minutes!

With all my love,
Chip

. . .

I get that nostalgia craving now. Before these letters came to life I went about my business without much thought of romance like walking hand in hand or gazing at a photo. Now I'm back there again. Your photos are out; in fact I have one right in front of me as I am writing. I'm looking at the one where you are writing to me from your bunk. You wrote on the back, *"Barb, I love you."*

Today, as I went walking there were couples walking hand in hand enjoying the day in the park. I thought I'd feel sad but instead I felt so happy for them. I wasn't alone. I felt your presence with me. There was a rock in the woods nestled between two trees with little pebbles fused into it. It had red speckles in it worn by the water's edge. I picked it up just when I was thinking about how your hand felt in mine. I held it on my way back home. Somehow, it felt like you were holding my hand through that rock.

When I'm told that someone has met their life partner at any age, I now feel giddy with excitement for them. It's an affirmation that love continues to exist all around me. I want them to feel what I felt with you. I want them to experience that solid foundation, trust and open heart that we had for each other. Possibilities are alive in every moment.

Sharing our story spreads delight and hope. Our partnership

still exists, just in a different form. I'm the luckiest gal for having you in my life.

LESSONS

Hi Love,

You are going to the Halloween party tonight. Have a good time. It should be a lot of fun; they usually are. What are you going as? Bobby is a good guy. I hope you remember to say hi to everyone. You can keep my spirit around there. At least one of us will be there.

As an answer to your question about you going I guess I could only explain it like this: It would hurt me if you didn't tell me. It would be definitely be an unexpected thing. I would be more shocked than anything else. I would ask you why you did it. Then my next question would be if you still loved me and only me. If you said no, naturally I'd get mad, I guess. If you said you still loved me, we would just have to sit down and talk about things.

I would not go out with anyone just because you did. That's a little out of line and anyway, it wouldn't help us get back together any sooner. That would be my main concern; getting back your love for me. If you had a reason for going out I wouldn't think any less of you. I know your reason wouldn't be to ease a want or desire. I wouldn't stop telling you I love you. I would want to say it more because I would wonder if you went out because you thought I didn't love you enough. I'd want to set it straight that I do love you dearly.

Babe, your word is gold to me. I believe you are mature enough to say what you feel. What you say is what I believe. When it comes to your feelings or actions, I believe only you. Other people can lie to me about things that happen; you wouldn't so I believe what you tell me. I always trust your judgment. One mistake couldn't change that. In short, not one or even a few mistakes could change any of my feeling for you. The only way is would is if you continuously tried to hurt me and make me not believe in you. I'm pretty sure that's the way things would turn out.

To be honest, right now I feel funny because you're going with Bobby tonight, not because of you and him (you're mine and Bobby's my friend, so no problem there), but because it's something that I really would have liked to take you. We would have so much fun at one of those parties. I just can't see you going without me. The picture can't get in my mind yet. I only see the two of us having fun. I guess it's hard for me to see it because I'm stuck here alone and everyone's there.

Stay with me forever and let us share all of our moments together, good or bad, happy or sad. I want to share them all with you. Together, things will be better. I must go now. Good night, love. I'll wake with thoughts of you.

I love you,
Chip

Whoa! Do I detect jealousy; a flaw? Nice surprise, in a way. You tumbled down off that pedestal I put you on. So, you were human after all! I could vision that lip curling smile like you just got caught with your hand in the cookie jar!

First of all, it was never a date and you knew that. I wish I could recall who Bobby was. What I do know is that it was one of your fireman friends and he was taking me to get me out of the house to enjoy the party at the firehouse.

That firehouse was always a safe haven for me; you all looked out for each other. They all knew how important we were to each other and would never infringe on our relationship or disrespect you in any manner. They wanted to include me and look after me, throughout and after your service. Your folks were going to be there, but at the end decided to stay home but encouraged me to go. And, you knew my devotion was only for you.

I'm glad you finished up by saying it was your sadness at not being with me and the gang that night. I would have gladly not gone if it would have hurt you. I'm sure we straightened it all out the next evening on our Sunday phone call. I can understand your frustration and emptiness away from home, your family and friends and me by your side. Half of our team only went to that party.

But, the greater lesson I received is how you worked it through by thinking and writing it out. We would have talked it over if we were together. The bigger gift was realizing that you would forgive me a transgression it if ever occurred. That largeness of your love is still unfathomable. I'm not sure I would have responded in the same manner.

Trust is the cornerstone of any relationship. That was, and still is, a cardinal rule. I never once mistrusted you and your sincerity. Being apart can put a strain on a relationship; but with us, it was just the opposite. Our letters brought us closer.

Many times when you were away and I was with friends, I couldn't wait to come home, read a letter, and replay all of our times together in my head. It brought me closer to you. Even now, sometimes I prefer your company from these letters. They bring me peace and joy. I feel as close to you now, as I did then.

RESPITE

Dearest Love,

It's Saturday afternoon. I have some time so I'm in the trees by the hut. I used to like to sit here during Basic so I figured I'd come here to write. It's nice and cool under this tree. It would be a nice place for the two of us to sit. I can think a lot here. It's so much a place for us that I can feel your presence. I can "talk" to you when I sit here. It's a place that we would come to relax and talk.

It's quiet-only the cars and people can be seen, but not heard. The trees are spaced out and it's a relatively open area. It's very peaceful. I can almost enjoy myself here. You would like it. I know

I would if we could be physically together. We're together now but only in a mental state. It's a close step to reality.

I may be away from your touch, but I'm very close to your heart. I know how much you love me. I love you just as much. I can feel your love coming to my heart every moment we're apart. You have all my love and total devotion.

Love & Kisses (many, many, many kisses)
Your husband,
Chip

. . .

You could be very involved in whatever you were doing and always found time for contemplation. You used to tell me work and money isn't everything. What's important is being happy with the simple things.

It's not that you didn't enjoy the stuff of life, but you always knew your priorities. We took drives to rural places upstate New York. You always liked quiet and peaceful discoveries where we could be alone surrounded by nature. You were infatuated with all creatures we encountered. I think you saw yourself as part of it; not separate from it.

You took great pleasure in sharing your discoveries with me. I was a willing student. Remember, I was a born a city gal, so this was a pleasant departure, especially through your eyes. My natural instinct, honed by the city streets, was to take the lead. With you, I was an equal partner in our adventures.

Nature has become so more important to me in these past years. I crave the trees and the sea, the mountains and gardens. I love planting flowers and vegetables and watching how they respond to the sun and the rain. When I sit in the garden to think, read or write, I feel the same peace you had felt. I gain perspective. It's one of my "happy" places.

When I had to take down a tree in front of the house because it split from a storm I kept some of the wood chips and placed them around another tree. Somehow, I believe it lives on. You would have done the same. There's another tree in its place now, growing strong and tall witnessing my life through the windows as I write to you now.

OWNERSHIP

Hi Babe,

Only 50 more days till I'll be home! Monday, we fired bazookas. It was very interesting. They're accurate and easy to shoot and a lot of noise. Then we shot grenade launchers. It's like a shotgun with a 2" diameter barrel. They have a nice kickback. Tuesday, we had landmine warfare and boobytraps. That was a little boring but something that had to be learned. Today I shot the big machine gun. It was a wild feeling. All these weapons are unbelievable.

I might go to N.C.O. school after AIT. It's a fairly good deal. It's a 3 month course to become an "instant sergeant." They asked me yesterday. I told them I needed to think about it. They gave me one minute to think. I had to say no. I couldn't do anything else without sleeping on the idea. They said that my answer will be changed if the Army says they want me. I might be ordered to go. I don't care either way. If they ask me again I think I'm still going to say no. They keep reminding us that we are the property of the U.S. Army. They don't know I belong to you.

I must go now. I'll write again as soon as I get a chance. I'll be home as soon as soon as possible.

I Love You,
Chip

As I was reading about your artillery training I had a vision of you as a young boy playing with trucks and guns and all those toys making noise, feeling delighted with the power it evoked. As an adult you still had fun with it, taking it in stride. It wouldn't become a daily activity for a few more months. Then it would become serious business.

It must be hard to lose independence in a military setting. It's hard enough in any setting. Every day you are reminded that you belong to someone else but yourself. It's a necessary consequence of military training. But, underneath, the essence of who we are is untouched if we protect it.

I think of Viktor Frankl's book, *Man's Search for Meaning*, and how as a Nazi prisoner in a WWII concentration camp he kept his sanity by staying true to his purpose and envisioning his future separate from his intolerable circumstances.

In some small way, I think you had to go into your deeper self to stay mentally afloat. Your very limited alone time and vivid mental images helped you. I was glad to play a part in it for you. I was your anchor to the outside world. I could bring you warmth and loving nourishment. I could mentally stand guard with you. I could soothe your aching muscles with my words. I realize now what an important part I played in your life. In the past I thought it was the other way around.

MUSIC

Hi Love,

How are things today? It's nice out here today. It's sunny and hot; a nice day for a drive. That's what I'd be doing now if we were together. It's a nice thought anyway. I like my thoughts and ideas. They seem so realistic. Each day I can find out more and more new ideas. It's something to do aside from missing you.

Blood, Sweat & Tears in on the radio. "And When I Die" is playing. Great song! I really like it, especially the harmonica. I should have brought mine with me. I should have brought you with me! Send yourself down in a package for me. I miss you so much.

Friday I get paid. Saturday I buy my ticket home. It'll be good to have that little piece of paper. It makes home a lot closer. Time together is coming fast if I'm buying my ticket already; 26 more days. Soon the countdown will be starting. I've been counting since July 15th! I'm on the way home, Babe. Just hang on tight. Keep the love flowing my way.

I Love You,
Chip

. . .

Ah, music! How it evokes memories! Scientists say that music can trigger the part of the brain that remembers explicit events that provoke emotion. We both were musically attuned. We enjoyed sharing our albums and listening to the "tunes" of the late 60's and singing along.

I remember the day you brought home the Beatles White Album. I think we wore it out! We had a lot of laughs with some of the songs, especially when you acted some of them out!

When we first heard Blood, Sweat & Tears, "You Made Me So Very Happy," we looked at each other and didn't have to say a word. The song said it all. It became our anthem. It still provokes a tear or a smile on my face.

You were right about the harmonica. They were a different rock group. They started incorporating jazz influences into their music. In fact, years later, I saw Randy Brecker with his brother, Michael play in a café in Greenwich Village. It was a great night.

When David Clayton-Thomas's haunting voice joined the band, his vocals penetrated my soul. That album came out the month we met. Whenever I hear our song, *God Bless the Child, I Love You More Than You'll Ever Know* or *Sometimes in Winter*, vivid memories comes to mind.

You would like it very much that now we can stream music

on our phones or speak into a tiny speaker and ask for the music of our choice. I have an eclectic playlist: classical, jazz, Motown, rock, R & B, country and even some opera. I'm open to all of it. I'm never without music. Life, for me, is dull without it.

SACRIFICE

Hi Babe,

We had a 1 ½ mile compass course tonight. It would have been easy except that it was through a swamp. Your Chip was running around in water for 2 hours. I was wet up to my knees. I didn't mind it until they made us stand in formation for 2 hours after we finished. Eight guys got lost and we had to wait until they were found. It's cold here at night now and my wet legs felt like icicles.

Tomorrow should be just as bad. I'll probably get in trouble for falling asleep during class. I did today and I know 4 hrs. of sleep won't help me out. They'll make me do P.T. and run again. I had to do that today but I really didn't care and I won't tomorrow either. I only have 17 more days.

There's nothing I want except you. I can't wait to get home. You better be careful. I'm going to smother you with love and kisses. It will be a new world for me. Instead of writing and telling you of my love, I'll be able to speak of it to you. As with everything, it's easier to show, then tell.

You mean the world to me. I'll sacrifice anything for your love. Soon we'll be together to unlock our hearts and let our love flow freely between each other. It's been a very long and hard time for both of us. I'm glad and extremely proud that we're still so much in love. I'm proud of you, Barb. I realize it's hard on you too. You sacrifice a lot for my love. I'll make it all up to you.

Love Forever,
Chip

. . .

The dictionary defines sacrifice as an act of offering to a deity something precious, especially the killing of a victim on an altar; destruction or surrender of something for the sake of something else, or something you give up or lose for someone else.

None of those definitions applied to us; at least not to me. The only thing we gave up was distance. We still held each other closely in our hearts. The act of love made it easy to work within the challenges of miles between us.

We didn't have to give up our freedom. Honesty balanced our individual needs with our combined dreams. We disagreed on some things from time to time but we were always able to come to the middle feeling like we never lost anything. We gained insight into each other and the world around us. You listened to my practical side; I absorbed your generous use of time and words.

Now, when I take the time to just sit and read or take a late afternoon nap after a cup of tea, I think of you. I no longer feel like I should be doing something more "productive." My thoughts naturally rearrange themselves into cogent messages. When I laugh and play I feel your exuberance and I'm young again, this time with no filters. My heart is lighter.

I can't think of a single thing I sacrificed for having you in my life. I'd do it all again without question. Your love has been the most enduring aspect in my life. I've just been reawakened by the memories. I'm still that gal holding your hand, sitting on the grass, tickling your ear and laughing at your funny expressions. You deserved all I had to give you; nothing less. What you gave me will last a lifetime.

FAITH

Dearest Love,
    How is everything with you? It's only 19 days away now. I still can't believe we're apart for so long. We're so close in love, yet so far away in distance. I must admit that I do pray each day for you and that you can feel the love I send to you.
    When I get home we have so much to do and not much time to get it all in. We'll have to spend all of our time together. We have a lot of past and future things to celebrate and don't forget all those kisses we owe to each other!
    We will be spending our one year anniversary together when I come home. It's good that we'll be together to mark one year. One day we will be celebrating another one year anniversary—only that will be our first wedding anniversary. You have made me so very happy during this year. I never knew how great life could be. You showed me the greatest things in life. I never before experienced love but now I'm filled with love for you.
    For 11 months we've loved with every beat of our hearts. Never in these 11 months have I had a bad moment; even here, I still enjoy with all my heart our love. That can never be taken away from me. My love for you is eternal. It will be with me when I die and remain with my soul in heaven.
    True love,
    Chip

You wrote to me about prayer on several occasions. We never really spoke about religion, but I knew you had faith and I was touched by your consistent prayers for me. As for death and eternity, I knew there was always the possibility, but I never expected it to be an imminent reality. You believed in the certainty about life beyond this physical realm. I wasn't so sure.
    In my family, life and death converged. We went to wakes,

funerals and cemeteries before we could walk. The dead were always remembered and even celebrated, particularly around the holidays. But, as casual as it was with family, I didn't want to broach that subject with you. For me, life after death was too complicated an equation: heaven, hell, purgatory or limbo. I wasn't sure where I would wind up so I avoided the subject entirely.

When you died I questioned everything I was told about faith and prayer. I had ten years of Catholic school. I was a prayer warrior. I believed that if enough prayers went up, good vibes would return. My simplistic belief system was shattered. I was mad at God for a very long time. I felt betrayed.

Didn't I pray enough? Did I falter somehow and that's why you were taken? Did I do some bad things and I was being punished? Wasn't I good enough to get my prayers answered? Did I not deserve your love? Who is this sadistic God that gives and then takes away? Every idiosyncratic religious tenet I learned was shaken. My spirit became barren.

Through the ups and downs of life after you I had glimpses of a greater spirit. The night my mother died in the hospital she was in and out of a coma in the last stages of cancer. I saw her unresponsive body and ashen skin. I went to the nurses' station and asked how she was doing? They advised she would be moving to hospice care. They told me her vitals were still strong but her passing would be soon. When I walked back to the room the monitor flat-lined, her skin illuminated and she had a smile on her face. This all happened in a matter of minutes.

I caught sight of something greater than death. However, the emptiness persisted. A piece of me was missing. It took me several years to discover what that was.

PICTURES

Hi Babe,

    The last three days and nights we had RVN (Nam) training. It was mostly walking and digging. We slept in foxholes which we dug. The weather was definitely against us, especially last night. At 3 a.m. this morning it was 5 degrees. I woke up and my canteen was all frozen.

    Last night was the worst. I thought it would never end. Naturally, we made our own fun. It breaks up the difficult times. Think only of the good times—that's my thinking.

    I got those pictures you sent me. They came out great. You're looking as beautiful as ever. Every time I look at any of your pictures, I just want to run into your arms, hold you and give you a big kiss. Soon, Babe; it's less than a week away when it will come true.

    Eternal Love,
    Chip

I look at your photos now. There aren't many but each one tells a story. Although photos bring back memories they never truly convey what is going on inside the mind and heart of a person. Is there worry, uncertainty or even mischief behind the smile?

    I go over every detail and, I too, wish they could come alive and tell me your thoughts at the moment of the camera click. A photo can only capture a second in time. I've taken so many of them over the years, especially of the places I've visited. But, we can't go back and relive those seconds. They stay frozen in time. They are captured images but limited in scope. They are just projections for the viewer.

    Everything is always changing. You can shoot a beautiful sunset over and over and in a matter of seconds it looks a bit different in each frame. Our thoughts and feelings are like that.

One minute we are thinking one thing and the phone rings and we are on to the next thing. We awaken feeling like we can take on the world and then a piece of mail gets delivered that can sour that bright outlook.

Your photos are a comforting friend without the dialogue. But, in some strange way they are telling me something more about you. You wanted me to be a part of your life between the miles and you wanted me to really see you, not parts, but all of you. You let me in without pretense. You trusted me with your heart and soul. It was the imperfections that you showed me that made you authentic. I was a privileged witness. I only hope that I was just as revealing to you.

HOME

Hi Love,

When you get this letter it will be in the final countdown. Come Friday I'll be "combat ready." That's what they say anyway. I hope it's true. I'll be seeing Nam pretty soon so I'll find out how much this training has helped.

I hope time goes fast, especially being overseas. Things will be a little tougher because of the mail. It's hard to write over there. We will make the most of our time together and talk over everything before I leave.

Are you ready to see me as a GI? I doubt it. No one will be ready for that. You'll probably be shocked that you will forget to kiss me! I hope I don't scare the love out of you. I know that will never happen. Our love is too strong and everlasting.

Soon I can tell you that I love you in person and I can hear you tell me of your love. I can't say I'm waiting patiently because I'm very impatient. I should land at 7:50 p.m. after a hold over in Atlanta. I'll call you from Atlanta to make sure I'm getting on the flight. That will give you plenty of time to get everyone together and get to the airport. I want to get to you as fast as possible.

Hang on Babe, I'll get there. I'm coming home to you. Be ready with that kiss.

Everlastingly yours,
Chip

. . .

The three weeks you were home were a whirlwind of activities. One of the first things you wanted, besides me, was serious Italian food which we ate a lot of at our favorite restaurants and at my house. Suddenly life was full and exciting again. There were plays, parties, friends, family, walks, movies; all the things we loved. Everyone was so happy to see you and to be with us and our plans for our marriage.

My classes were almost over and I took off from work so we could spend as much time as possible together. We squeezed a year into three weeks. We talked about everything and we prepared as best as we could for our year separation. We felt the warmth between us and clung to each other as much as possible.

A few days before you left we took a ride upstate to enjoy the countryside and to relish the peace and quiet of alone time together. As we approached Albany, you looked over at me and said, *"let's keep going, all the way to Canada and get married."* That was the third time you proposed. This time you wanted to make it happen.

I remember feeling caught between the strong desire to say "yes" and the chains that bound me to family expectations. We pulled over, held each other and didn't speak for a while. We knew it would be a decision that wouldn't be reversed.

Like everything else, we discussed it from all angles and finally decided that we would disappoint our families if we didn't do it formally with them. We still had our vows we made to each other. We decided to wait till you returned and get formally engaged when you went on R&R midway into your deployment.

Many years later when I saw your mother she told me that she and your Dad had wished we had eloped when you were home. I smiled and remembered how much courage it took not to do it. She said that they always thought of me as their daughter with or without the certificate. Your family showed me so much love then and afterwards for which I am eternally grateful.

Knowing how difficult it would be to be apart we promised each other that whenever either one of us got sad or scared we would somehow know and smile for each other to ease the pain. We would have to read between the lines in our letters when it got difficult. We would stay strong for each other.

You left on Sunday, December 14, 1969. That was the last time I held you in my arms and felt your heart beat next to mine.

*It's not the load that breaks you down,
it's the way you carry it."*
~Lou Holtz

VIETNAM

(DECEMBER 1969 - MARCH 1970)

POSTAGE

Hi Babe,

    It's 12:15 in the afternoon here in California. I'm leaving here tomorrow and will be landing in Bien Hoa after stopping in Hawaii, Okinawa and the Philippines. Bye, Bye U.S.A! See you next year! All together, we'll be flying for 22 hours.

    I'm in a small group here made up of all artillery. I finished processing early this morning. We were taken to our barracks at 6 a.m. and we were given 1 hour to fix our bunk, clean ourselves and sleep. As you can tell, I still haven't slept since I left home. I now have all of my jungle clothes. When I turned in my dress uniform, I'm glad I found your pictures in one of my pockets. I forgot they were there.

    Babe, I want to thank you for the greatest three weeks of my life. Every moment is one I'll always remember. As I left, I brought along memories enough to last forever. I've been keeping my head so far. I'm half smiles. Don't forget our promise.

    This will probably be my last letter with a stamp. Once you see "free" written on the envelope you know where I am. It will probably be a week or so before you hear from me again. Letters will take a while to get to you. Don't worry. I'll be writing. Blame it on the mailmen! Keep on smiling.

I love you
Chip

. . .

I wish I could have memorized every moment we spent together during those three weeks, but time and memory won't cooperate. I do remember how empty I felt when you left. I could feel the distance grow from here to California and then on to the other side of the world.

The postage on your stateside letters was six cents in 1969. So much love came from those letters. We got our money's worth. Now, for you, they would be free. But, was it? There is always a price. The price of war is unfathomable. I call it the long arm of war. I wrote this piece 24 years after you died.

> The lover of the soldier is torn within the paradox
> Our insides wretch with guilt
> Hate war, love the beloved
> When you return,
> Alive or dead
> You are never as you were before
> War has no victors, only survivors
> Picking up the pieces of humanity's host
> How many lives have been shattered to the wind?
> When you go to war
> You do not go alone
> In the silence you may know who we are
> But survival is the matter at hand
> When you tell your stories
> Please understand
> There is a long arm to war

. . .

A stamp merely pushes an envelope from one place to another. There is always a price for freedom.

FOREIGN SOIL

Hi Babe,

I arrived and am in Long Bien now. We passed the International Date Line, so I never saw Wednesday. I'm assigned to the 25th Infantry Division, Tropic Lightning. It operates in the Mekong Delta. It's the one company no one wants to be in. They're always in the swamps and rice paddies. I'll be reporting to them late this afternoon or early tomorrow.

It's dirty and very poor living here. I really feel sorry for the people. I bought a camera and I'm going to be sending a lot of pictures home. You can see for yourself. We got all our money converted. This stuff looks funnier than Monopoly money. It's all paper. The colors are wild. It's military currency, not Vietnamese.

We can't drink any water. It's all polluted. We can only drink the water from big trucks (oil trucks) filled with treated water. There are constantly at least 5 or 6 helicopters flying overhead real low. They are always coming and going to the field. When we landed a flare shot up and a machine gun cut loose. What a feeling! It turned out to be nothing.

By my calculations by the time you get this it will be Christmas so I better say, "Merry Christmas, I love you." Take care of yourself. I'll be home December 16, 1970, the latest!!

I love you,
Chip

Well, it was now real. You were in Vietnam; a whole different part of the world. In many of your letters you wrote about coming back to the world, meaning home. Vietnam was a destination, not the real world.

I suppose reframing the environment gave you comfort so you could straddle the two places in your psyche to cope with the separation from everything you knew. I wonder, as time moved on, if home took on a different perspective. Our mission was to keep reminding you of what was waiting for you through our letters and packages.

Everything took on a new meaning. Clean drinking water, shelter from the rain, a firm mattress, familiar currency—all of it so familiar to me was now an altered reality for you. I collected an assortment of boxes, preparing to send you packages filled with "home."

Both of us came from working families and we didn't take much for granted. We were prepared to work hard for what we wanted in life. However, we were now in uncharted waters. Comfort was not an option. We had to live in a parallel universe. Distance was more than a line between two geographical points. We were living in two different places on the planet. No more weekly phone calls. The only way we would communicate for the next year was through our letters and possibly an occasional recorded tape. This was a new test for the both of us. Somehow, we were willing to make it work.

OBSERVATIONS

Hi Barb,

I'm now in Cu Chi. It's real war-like here. They have a lot of artillery and armor. The big artillery guns keep going off every few hours all night. The machine guns also cut loose. They are very loud and wake me up at night. We also have a helicopter landing right next to our barracks. They come in at night and also wake me up. It's all part of the game.

I stay here for 7 to 10 more days. After here, I go to Tay Ninh which is approximately 20 miles NW of Saigon. Tay Nihn is called Rocket City. They always get hit with rockets. It's near a mountain, a jungle and unfortunately rice paddies. Oh well. Soggy feet!

I found out the job of the company I'm going to. It's a fire base operating directly from Tay Ninh. We go out for 3-7 days. Our job is to stop the enemy from getting supplies from Cambodia. We're located on the Cambodian border most of the time. There's a big North Vietnamese headquarters a few miles from our temporary camp. That's what we were told today. That can change at any time.

I like my gun. It fires great–no problems yet. We should have a good year together. It had been shot once or hit by shrapnel. There's a hole in the hand guard and a big dent on the heat deflector. It should know what to do. It can teach me. It has more experience. It's a newer model, too.

I had to go through the gas chamber today. It was a high concentration of tear gas. It was pretty bad with the heat. All my pores were open and my whole body burned. The burning lasts about 15 or 20 minutes. Forget about my eyes. They were tearing for about 10 minutes. It's all part of the training. I finish training Christmas day.

The TET offensive starts about January 6th or so and lasts until January 16th or 18th. Everyone's getting ready for that now. They're clearing a lot of space around the perimeter here so they can see when Charlie attacks. Sir Charles is after this place and also Tay Ninh. There's a story behind it.

Tay Ninh is the seat of the major religions in Vietnam. North Vietnam believes that if they can control it, they can get the people all over Vietnam helping the north for fear of losing their religion and their gods. Last year during TET they tried twice to take Tay Ninh, but unfortunately they lost 700 men in the process. They *fought on and off for 2 days and finally gave up. Now, they figure that they will try again.*

Last year during TET the 4th BN, 9th INF fought for 3 days in an outstanding victory. They supposedly lost one man and the North Vietnamese lost over 100. Everyone says the unit I'm assigned to is a real good unit. There's nothing to worry about. We have a lot of Vietnamese working with us. They are good at finding booby traps and also at searching the underground tunnel complexes. Both are very dangerous, but they do it.

Take care, Barb, and remember you hold my heart in your hands (don't squash it!). I love you with all my heart. Keep your spirits high and your love flowing my way. Together we can make it. We have to help each other through this. SMILE! Come on— now that's better!

Forever & devotedly yours,
Chip

. . .

Cu Chi, Tay Ninh, Cambodian tunnels—those were places in the news, now you were there. It seemed so surreal that you were writing about these places as the news back home mentioned them on a daily basis. Most of the news was disastrous and caused great anxiety. It was the first war that was captured on television as it was happening.

You made it sound as casual as if it was a new job in a new place. I guess, it was from your perspective. If I was a journalist or an unbiased observer, it would sound quite interesting. However, those names evoked fear in me at the time. You were somewhere in the middle of it. Without the immediacy of communication every patrol or skirmish had the possibility to take you away from me. How could I not worry?

I wonder if you would find it amusing now that Vietnam has a strong economy and is a tourist attraction. There are skyscrapers in Ho Chi Minh City and Hanoi. Yup, they have adventure and luxury tours, golf courses, resorts and beautiful beaches. I eat Vietnamese food and sometimes I see clothes manufactured in their thriving factories. The U.S. and Vietnam now have mutual economic and security interests. There was great suffering to the Vietnamese people caught up in a relentless civil war. I'm glad that some good has come out of it.

Isn't it ironic that after so many battles and bloodshed through the ages that trade, travel and political partnerships prevail? Does time heal all wounds? Maybe, it's just human nature to break up and make up. But, when you were there, I was only interested in the day I would no longer hear the names of those places.

I actually would be interested in traveling there; not for a morbid reason, but to experience it through my own eyes. That is why I enjoy travel so much. I want to avail myself of the uniqueness of the people and places I visit. I don't want to borrow other people's biases and expectations. I need to make my own observations and decisions. We agreed that experience is the best teacher. That's how you viewed your deployment. It took me far more many years to embrace that maxim.

MELANCHOLY

Hello Love,

I'm back from the field. I love you dearly! I can't get my mind off of you. I want you so much. It's really hard being here. I'm not looking for any easy way out, but if you were here, half the problems would be over.

I miss you more than anything. Being away from you bothers me more than having to go out to the filed looking for Charlie. I'll say one thing. Those 2 days in the field went by like about 2 hours. Time goes by fast. Out there I don't think of you as much.

It sounds terrible, but I always think of you here on base. Out there I think of getting home to you. It's a lot different. It's better thinking of getting home to you than thinking only of you and wishing I was home. I'm more on the ball when I know I'm going to come home to you. It's something to be careful about, yet it eases my mind.

I was glad I naturally thought like that yesterday and the day before. I was worried that I'd always be daydreaming of you and not thinking about what I'm doing. It's better not to think of you. It's like sleeping and if something happens you cannot react. I hope you understand what I mean.

Sorry about all of this, but I'm so lonely for you. I feel so empty. There's a lot going on, but all I want is you. There are so many memories to keep me going. I'm glad we did everything we did while I was home. I feel so much closer to you. I didn't think we could get any closer than we were, but it brought us closer yet. You mean so much to me.

I just got two more letters from you. Thanks for all the mail. Write as much as possible. I like hearing from you. Take care, Babe. I love you. You're all mine and I'm all and only yours.

Love Always,
Chip

. . .

I understand what you mean about being able to focus on everyday life when I'm reading these letters from you, reliving memories and writing back to you now.

Sometimes, I just want to make a cocoon from your letters and feel your love surrounding me. It's a great comfort to lose myself in the past when the present isn't so lovely. A peace comes over me from your words and remembering your smile warms my heart. But, then life beckons and I'm busy doing what needs doing and you are sidelined for a while.

When I'm doing my counseling work, working on my art pieces or surrounded by others I'm temporarily distracted. I'm focused on the immediate. But, you are always there in the back of my mind and even though you are with me in spirit I, too, feel the emptiness of your voice and touch. It's one thing to know something; it's another thing to feel it in present time.

Thoughts of what could have been seep into my mind and the remapping of my life if you would have returned to me makes me wonder how different my life would have been. I know it's a slippery slope to do that, but how could I not think about it from time to time?

I am very content with my life as it is and generally happy. I've had many adventures and wonderful people in my life along with the proverbial ups and down. I've been fortunate in so many ways. What I miss is the family we would have had. I wish your nephews knew their uncle. I wish my niece and nephew got to know you. I wish I would have grown old with you and laughed, cried and even argued with you.

We balanced each other so very well. I have not found that balance since you were gone. Then, I think of what you would say when I'm in that melancholy mood—*"Babe, It's not that bad. You know I will always love you. Come on smile. There, that's better."*

ADAPTATION

Hi Babe,

I just back from that patrol I went on. I've never been so scared before. We were set up across the river from a North Vietnamese base camp. They were making noise all night. Thank God we didn't make any contact. They would have nailed at least half of us. We could hear their every move and even heard them talking. One of them fell into the river and started hollering. He was a few hundred yards up the river from us.

It rained the whole time we were out. I was soaked from the minute we landed. For two nights I had to sleep in the rain with nothing over our heads—not even a tree!

> I got three more letters from you today and the one with your nail in it. I put it in my wallet with your picture. Now I have a piece of you with me. You must understand how much I love you. I couldn't get along without you. I feel so empty when we are apart, yet so full of the love that you give me each and every day. I will always be yours. Nothing could stop that. We make each other's lives complete.
>
> Here's a little prayer I found that I really like. It's called A Prayer for a Girlfriend. Here goes:
>
> "Take care of my girl, dear God. You know her so well. Help her understand the absences caused by my duty. Help us both be good, pure and faithful during this time. Strengthen her from temptations and guard her from the dangers from which I cannot now shield and protect her. Above all, dear God, if it is your will that the beautiful friendship we now share grows into still deeper love, please then, guide us both in our free choice of one another so that it is based on trust and love. Yes, dear God, I love her. She is really my best girl. Please take care of her and thanks, God—it's so good just to have someone so special as her."
>
> That says just about everything. I love you. Hang in there. Have faith. I'll be there looking only for you.
>
> Forever Yours
>
> Me

· · ·

As an avid reader I've read books and seen plenty of war time movies. I don't know why they fascinate me. Being a lover of history, I'm always looking to learn something from the past. It took me a long time to read or see a Vietnam movie but when I did I got a sense of what it must have been like for you to be in the jungle and rice paddies.

I think adaptation is the key. It's amazing what one can do when thrust in a new and challenging environment. You have the fear but you keep going. Military life is constant adaptation. I think that's how you survived on a daily basis.

Part of that adaptation for you was a deepening faith. I remember my father telling me how during WWII his orders were serendipitously changed the night before he was going to be sent to North Africa. His commander had returned and spoke with him that night to wish him well and after a discussion decided to have his orders changed. He was sent to the Pacific island of Guam just after the Marines had retaken it. Even though he was a sharpshooter, he never had to fire his gun in that war.

Most of the regiment that went to Africa never made it back. He believed it was divine intervention that changed the trajectory of his life. It's one of reasons he embraced his faith so fervently throughout his life. Chances are if he had gone to Africa I wouldn't have been born, we wouldn't have met and I wouldn't be writing this to you.

My faith has taken me on a circuitous path. After you died I couldn't find comfort in church. I went out of duty, but not based on faith. Years later I found myself searching and found myself at a retreat where I met a Jesuit who changed the way I thought about faith and introduced me to a much bigger world of spirituality.

I studied most world religions and have been to churches of different denominations, Jewish & Buddhist temples and even a mosque in Spain. I've gained an appreciation for the differences and the key similarities. My faith is in the divine spark that resides in each of us. I believe there is a oneness that connects us; even when we don't understand it. I think I had to lose religion to find God.

Do our lives travel on faith or destiny's road? I don't know. What I do know now is that I am more comfortable with the unknown and willing to travel on whatever road life takes me. Some might call it faith. I prefer to call it adaptation. Whatever the label, I embrace the mystery.

FIRE

Hi Babe,

 We just had a bad fire. The supply room, B company's orderly room, our weapons room and D company's orderly room burned right down to the ground. I got there before it left the supply room so I went into the orderly room to try to get all the records out. There were three of us in the back room and that went up too.

 A guy grabbed me by the neck from behind to get me out. When he did the chain broke and the medal you gave me fell off. I didn't have time to get it. The rooms are made from bamboo strips and they burned very fast. I had to get out quickly.

 The fire department came and they were a real comedy, just like slapstick. They are Vietnamese civilians with lousy equipment. They were falling over everything. Then they ran out of water. When they got water, it only shot about 5 feet from the nozzle. I had to laugh.

 We lost a lot—15 rifles, one 50 caliber machine gun, a few M-60 machine guns, grenade launchers and starlight scopes costing from $3,000 and up each. They lost 3 - 5 of them. They had three $50,000 scopes in there that are gone. There was also a lot of ammo in there and it all went off. It was a real bad deal.

 After the fire, I went in the ruins and looked for the medal. I didn't expect to find it, because walls, ceilings and everything were lying around. I didn't see it. It's definitely gone.

 Tomorrow at 5:00 a.m. we're going on patrol. It's said that we'll be there three nights. I'll write while I'm out there. I'll let you know how I feel (probably scared as hell!)

 I love you. Take care. You have all my love and devotion. Smile!!!

 I'll Love You Forever
 Chip

. . .

Your fireman's instincts drew you into that burning building, wanting to save what you could. It was your natural inclination. On several occasions we would be on our way to or from something and we would see a car stuck on the side of the road and you would stop and help the person to fix a tire or give a ride to make a phone call. You sprung into action without question.

I wasn't surprised that you ran into that fire. It's a good thing that it probably took over a week to get the letter telling me about it and that you lived to tell the tale. While I understood your behavior I didn't want you to be a hero and jeopardize your life. On the flip side, it's one of the things I loved about you. You were the guy to be counted on to show up. That saying, '*actions speak louder than words*' definitely applied to you.

As for the lost medal, I guess it didn't matter. It did what it was supposed to. It saved you from the fire. I replaced it and sent it with the peace sign on a leather chain you requested. In addition to your dog tags, you had a medal and a peace talisman to cover all the bases.

It reminds me of one of the messages in the Bhagavad-Gita, a Hindu scripture. It's a dialogue between a warrior prince, Arjuna, and the god Krishna before Arjuna goes into battle. Lord Krishna tells him *"plunge into the heat of battle and keep your heart at the lotus feet of the Lord."* It's about the battles in life. We can do our duty with all out heart but not get attached to the outcome. Our soul doesn't get destroyed even if our body perishes.

When I first read that line about 20 years after you departed, I first remembered how you handled war and wrote the most beautiful, loving letters with the same breath. I also applied it to my own life in a myriad of ways. It's one of my favorite spiritual reminders. The scripture has been a saving grace for me through life's difficulties.

I wasn't thinking about that line when I recently placed your picture in the frame with a Hindu Buddha watching over you. I guess that was *my* natural inclination.

LOGISTICS

Hi Love,
   I'm out in the field now. I got your medal yesterday. It's real nice. Thanks a lot. I felt bad when I lost the other one. It had a lot of meaning and love in it. It still does, even though I no longer have it. I have all the memories that we have shared with it.
   I'll give you the whole thing on me. I'm in Tay Ninh base camp. It's right next to Tay Ninh City. The city is right at our gate. We're N.W. of Saigon. We have a certain area of operation. I'll try to get a map and put down where we are and where we work. I'm not there all the time–only to rest. We go different places and set up ambush sites. My job is to shoot up Charlie. I'm full core infantry.
   Every time we go out we're looking to kill the enemy. Tay Ninh is fairly close to Black Virgin Mt. It's about 3-5 miles from the base. It has a lot of companies in it. The company you read about was from here. It was called the Regulars.
   When we go out we usually go as a company. We split up in the field to platoon size ambushes. We keep within 1000 meters from each other. The platoon splits up into squads and set up a sort of circle. It all ties in so your rear is covered. No one can get into the circle because the lines of sight and fire intersect. You can think of it as a fence. We usually set up 3 platoons like that. The 4th platoon is the mortar platoon and they set up farther away with the company commander and his people.
   Now we are set up in Renegades Woods, about 1000 meters from the Cambodian border. I'm carrying a radio this time. I have to stay with it at all times in case someone tries to call us. It

weights 30 lbs. but the pack adjusts so I can get it into a comfortable position.

There are a lot of bugs here. There are a lot of bugs everywhere in this country! Last night two mosquitoes were going to eat me alive. They are really big!

All yours in love and devotion,
Your Chip

. . .

I'm surprised that your mail wasn't censored. You were able to provide so many details about your location and assignments. I guess they weren't worried about interceptions. In that letter you drew a picture of how the platoons were set up. Your engineering studies and analytical skills were imported into precise diagrams.

The details helped me to understand what your day was like. My letters were filled with what was going on day-to-day with me and what was happening with our friends and families. The exchanges of daily activities made us feel closer to each other. I admit I was more afraid of your activities than you were of mine.

I enjoyed sharing books we enjoyed and writing about them or working on crossword puzzles together. It created a linkage and a sense of normalcy as if you were near. There were times when I wrote about something I was thinking about and a letter would arrive dated the same as the letter I wrote to you with the same thoughts. Our minds were telepathically attuned. I got so much joy over that.

I also sent you newspaper clippings of battles and activities reported from Vietnam for you to comment. In 1969, a lot of activity was at the Cambodian border and I followed the news which was a blessing and curse. I was always concerned about what mission you were on and if you were involved. The time lag between our letters could be a week to 10 days.

You made it sound like you had it all under control so as not to alarm me but you couldn't protect me from the reported facts and daily statistics. As for the bugs, everyone liked you so wouldn't the bugs also be drawn to you?

PERCEPTIONS

I love you, Barb!

I got your package today. Thanks, I can use all of it. It took about 8 days to get here. Everything was in one piece, nothing dented or crushed. I also found two letters from you when I got in.

Don't worry about what you hear on the radio. So far, nothing has happened to us. I'll write if anything does. The 25th is a good sized outfit with lots of different battalions and companies. There is only a slim chance I'll ever be on anything you hear on the radio. I'll let you know when things get rough.

Yesterday, I went swimming in a bomb crater. It was mighty fine. The water was nice and cool. It was deep (about 9ft. in the middle). I was swimming around for about 45 minutes before I came out. I have a picture of me coming out which I'll send you.

I can tell already that it will take a lot of doing to get used to living in the world again. It's so different here. Back home there are bathrooms with flushing toilets and sinks. No such thing here. Here, you follow the Beatles song and "do it in the road."

Riding through villages you see men and women doing their thing off the side of the road. Small children only wear shirts, no bottoms, so if they have to go, they don't wet themselves. They just do their thing. Once out of camp, we all do the same thing. It's life over here.

It's nothing to curse out anybody here, man or woman. The English the people know is all stuff with curses. If you know Vietnamese they don't try to explain in it an easier way. It's just a "go to hell" or a lot worse. Little kids either give us the peace sign or just one finger. Some don't know the difference, but most do. Some guys just cannot get used to it.

It's definitely a war worth fighting. It will better the people. It's something they want, but won't admit. Support it! It's doing a lot of good. No war is worth lives lost, but it's a thing that must happen. There are a lot of people here who worship the GI's and the USA for the help we're giving them. The goodness does definitely outweigh the bad as I see it.

Most of the people back home are against it only because they're too afraid of getting hurt. They don't know what they're talking about. I didn't either, which is one reason I wanted to come here. You can't believe other people; you have to see for yourself and make up your own mind. There are guys here who differ with my views. We talk about it, argue and try to exchange our views.

Never believe anyone who wasn't in infantry or who never leaves the base camp and only hears stories. I'm not playing up the infantry in the fighting (I wish I was in the rear), but they experience and see the most action. They often work directly with the people. Sorry to bore you. I just got carried away.

I love you dearly. Don't worry about me. Everything will be fine. Take care and SMILE!

Love always,
Chip

. . .

I don't know what I wrote back to you about supporting the war. I only knew the first hand information from you to base what was happening there. But, even then I was ambivalent. I didn't pick a side, for or against, at that time. You wrote this letter only one month in. My views changed and this is where we now differ based on history and perspective.

Back home it was 1969 and the country was deeply divided and filled with unrest. Demonstrations, deceit, mistrust and frustration were fueled by the war, racial injustice and women's rights issues. Of course, people were scared and didn't want to be hurt. It was difficult to wrap our heads around why we were there and what appeared to be a never-ending "conflict." It was different from previous wars where the precursor was a concrete, response to direct confrontation.

The information we got was sketchy and filtered through a political lens. Many returning veterans came home physically and/or emotionally wounded and were virtually unsupported by both sides. There was vacillation between withdrawal and escalation. It's the war we would like to forget, but thankfully so many now remember the lives and sacrifices made during that period of time.

Afterwards, so much of this came out through investigations, especially the Pentagon Papers. Ideology or political gain creates wars, generals apply the tactical backbone and soldiers supply the muscle. I think it would be a fairer playing field if at least one member of every politician's family served in the armed forces. That would make their decisions more thoughtful and realistic. It is one thing to make decisions based on figures; it's another to deploy based on personal reality.

Back then, I didn't have the confidence or political savvy to express my view, nor did I have the personal experiences that you encountered. I mostly kept silent to avoid the subject entirely. I just knew our lives depended on what happened there and I supported you.

Ultimately, much later, the war did bring some stability to Southeast Asia and the future of Vietnam became promising. Isn't that true of most wars? Enemies later become allies. All I know is that the price of war is steep and we paid dearly for it. I do agree with you that experience is the best teacher. It would interesting to have been able to see how either of our views stood up against the test of time. Perceptions shift with the change in tides.

NAMES

Hi Babe,

Right now, I'm sitting in a wood line about 20 feet from an open field. I came back here early this morning to get shade so I could sleep. I'm sitting on my poncho liner. I have your name all over it so every night I can sleep with my wife. You're always with me. I have your name on everything that has my name on it: my hat, helmet and my boots, so you're always with me.

Love usually stems from a certain thing that appeals to someone. Well, as usual, I'm different. My love stemmed from only one thing. My love now is still based only on one thing—that is Barbara Cafiero, formerly Barbara Joan Spinelli!

Hon, as soon as we met you inspired me. Everything you had said and done set up a feeling inside of me. It was a funny feeling—one I never had—one I questioned until I saw you again. I found I couldn't get an answer so I started to analyze the whole thing. The first thing I came upon was that you were very mature. You knew your stuff and you were set in your ways, maybe, let's say, stubborn! You would fight back and never let anyone take advantage of you or do you wrong. I found you were honest and truthful and subtle at times, too.

All the time I was trying to figure things out, I felt I wanted to make you happy. That was all I wanted to do. That was new to me. It was a strange feeling. Making you happy, made me happy. That made no sense at the time. I just wasn't that kind of guy. I found I wanted to be with you rather than the boys. I looked forward to calling and seeing you. I saw a light and I really wanted to find out what we could make of our "friendship."

It started out that I would always think of you and just sigh. It grew stronger and stronger so we saw more of each other. I couldn't find anything that didn't appeal to me. I felt so much inside of me. I always thought of you before I did things. Then, I wanted to tell you all about me and my past. We had that long talk and I felt so easy with you. I was amazed at how I could talk *and feel so at ease. Well, I knew I loved you. I knew it was serious and I had to tell you. I was afraid that was a little too much to say, so I said I was sorry before I told you and then I figured I would never see you again.*

I never did find anything I don't like about you. You're everything I've ever dreamed of. We are happy together. I'll do anything to keep things like that. We have special things going for us. We have trust and love. I feel so at ease with you. You have a way of calming me. When we're together all I fell is our happiness and the flow of our love. When we're apart I feel a need for your presence. I'm always empty without you.

Love Always,
Your Chip

. . .

Ok, I have to take a few long breaths! So much to live up to! But, first, we had to get my middle name correct. I laughed about it, sent you a note back with my middle name and you sent back a funny apology. You weren't the first to get my middle name wrong. It's always been expected to be Jean or Joan. No one has ever guessed it correctly. I mostly only use the initial. Blame my mother. She was obsessed with Joyce. I never got the back story on that.

I loved having my name all over your stuff. I smile at that thought. My father did the same thing with his belongings. I think it shortens the distance between two people. I wore your shirt till it practically fell apart. I didn't want to wash it because I swore it had your perpetual scent on it. It's one of those funny things lovers do to keep things "real."

As for your thoughts of me, I can agree on the maturity comment. I came out of the womb prematurely, was walking and talking earlier than most, started first grade at the ripe old age of five and was helping out at home when my mother went to work when I started school. Some of it was wiring; some of it was environmental. I wish I could have gone to kindergarten and finger painted but I was thrust right into the ABC's early on with report cards right behind.

The discovery of first love is always a mystery. Past encounters are bland compared to the colors, sounds and touch of souls clicking. It feels foreign and exciting simultaneously. New words in one's vocabulary start to surface. Hours of questions circle inside our heads. The same thoughts you had were also inside of me. It was like getting on a roller coaster, frightening and thrilling but determined to stay on it for the ride.

Our relationship took me to places I would have never experienced before. However, I wasn't as self-assured as you thought I was. I was full of doubts of self worth. How can you love me so much when I know I'm not perfect (family script), was a familiar thought in my head.

Gradually our little faults emerged as we spent time together. Instead of faltering, our incompleteness made us more comfortable with each other. You were the first person I didn't have to be perfect for. Being myself became easier. You didn't run away and I didn't turn my back on you when you told me you loved me. Destiny stepped in. Forces beyond our control took over and the rest is a beautiful history.

GIFTS

Hi Babe,

Yesterday was a quiet birthday. Nothing much happened. Today, some of the guys gave me a C-ration pound cake with handmade icing on it. It had 20 matches on it. They made me blow them out. It was funny. They also gave me a pack of cigarettes.

The hardest part of being here is the fact that we are apart. Everything else is a physical strain, but that goes away fast. My love and want for you will never, ever leave me. The only thing that keeps me going is the fact that I know you are mine. We have our future to look forward to. This time apart will be only an old dream compared to all the time we will have to share.

Sorry I have to cut this so short. I have to go on patrol again tonight. I've been having radio problems so I better check things out before I leave. It's not a good thing when you are stuck in a rice paddy with no communication.

I love you—never forget that. Take care, Barb. Smile! I'm all yours and only yours. I'm yours through thick and thin, for better or worse.

Forever yours,
Your Loving Husband,
Chip

. . .

We missed another birthday together. Everyone on this end sent boxes of goodies and lots of cards and letters. I'm glad your buddies did what they could to celebrate with you. I'm sure you had more than a few laughs and some spirits to lift your spirits. I wish I could have spent your last birthday with you. I was there in spirit as I am now with you.

I am writing this on what would have been your 71st birthday. It's a grey day but my heart is full of love and light. Here's what I would be writing to you now:

My Dearest Chip,

I am so grateful that your parents joined together and brought you into the world. They gave me the greatest gift of love when you entered my life. You color my world with bright and subtle hues. The exciting times and the deeply intimate moments bring out sides of me that I didn't know I had. You breathed life into my heart.

I love you for that certain smile that cheers me when I'm blue. I love you for your tender kiss that warms my heart. I love you for your gentle hand and your eyes that always seem to say "I love you very much." I love you for your faith in me and your sweet and patient ways. I love you for your gift of words that express your deepest thoughts so well. I love you for the many caring things you do without seeking praise.

I love you, darling, for all these things and so much more. But most of all, I like me because of who I've become from being with you.

Happy Birthday!

With all the love that's always yours,

Your Barb

COMMUNICATIONS

Dearest Barb,

I love you, Babe! Not much is new here. I sent you all my love on a satellite last night. I see this satellite a lot on clear nights. It passes right by the little dipper (about 8:20 last night). I was looking for it. When I found it I put my love on it for you.

I know you can feel my love coming to you. I sure as hell can feel yours. It's mighty powerful! I can always sense your presence and feel your closeness to me wherever I am. It's a great feeling. Don't you agree?

The other night I got into my first night firefight. It was really weird. The flashes from the barrel are all we could see and they were only about 15 feet away. We ambushed them. There were five of us and ten of them. After about five minutes, five more guys came to help us. It lasted a long time. No one got hurt, but we got a V.C. captain. He was really bad off. They should just give up the war.

I just got put in for an Army accommodation medal for that ambush. It's not definite. They are reviewing it. The Lieutenant that put me in for it was reporting to me over the radio. He said I did a good job. I'm now permanent RTO (radio telephone operator). I'll find out about the medal in a month or two. That will look good on my record, getting one with such little time in the country. Even getting put up for one is something good on my record.

I'm writing by candlelight; sexy, isn't it? I'm eating a small box of corn flakes. I'll be right back.

They just made me blow out the candle. There were loads of V.C. in the area and they thought we might have a ground attack. I must go. I love you. Take care.

Devotedly yours,
Chip

Not much is new! Within 48 hours you managed to send your love on a satellite, engaged in a firefight, got recommended for an accommodation, became the permanent radio man and wrote to me by candlelight. You also left me hanging with a possible impending enemy attack!

My same two days probably included classes, work, coming home hopefully to a letter from you and writing back before lights were out on my end.

Our days were so different being apart. Before, we both were taking classes, working and spending as much time together in between. Now, you were working on staying physically alive and I was working on keeping my wits in check. Either way, we were both on the same track coming from opposite ends of the globe–getting back into each other's arms.

By the way, I was happy for you about the accommodation. However, it was for one encounter. I would have had a chest full of medals for all the romantic and loving gestures you shared with me. Radio man with a satellite; I'm still conjuring up the image in my mind.

I just blew out my candle. Good night, my love.

IMPATIENCE

I love you, Barbara!

I was dreaming of you before. It was so realistic. We were married and had a kid. His name was Richard. He was going to school, so I guess he was about 6 or 7 and he got in trouble and you had to go see his teacher. Let's get married!

I want to marry you soon, very soon! I could never be happy without you. My love is so great, Barbara, that I really cannot wait much longer before we are married. If things don't change when I come home, if this force keeps driving at me, we'll get married right after I get out.

I realize it would be harder and not as we have talked and planned, but I must have you for my wife. I'm going crazy being away from you. All I can think of is the tremendous amount of love I possess in my heart for you. I want to share this love with you 24 hours a day and be with you to share every feeling of joy, sorrow, love and desire. I want to share the good and the bad. It's a matter of being together while we are apart. I hope you feel the same way.

Till I get home all you have to do is seriously say you will be my wife and act as one till we are married in the church. I don't want to be your boyfriend or you, my girlfriend. We are so much a part of being married to each other already. Send me the ring. I'm really serious about this. Start changing the name on your license! I'm telling everyone that we consider ourselves married and they should consider it also.

Never underestimate how much I love you. It's great and very strong. Your love and presence makes me so very happy. I really enjoy every moment we've spent together. We fit together so well.

Take care and stay mine. I'll always be yours and yours alone. All I want, all I need, is YOU!

Yours forever,
Your Chip

. . .

I can only imagine how overwhelmed I felt when reading this because even now it makes my heart beat faster. Not all of it is because of your proclamation. Some of it is because of the urgency you expressed. It's not you I doubted; it was the circumstances behind it. Were you scared, sad or just in a lonely or passionate mood?

A group of guys living minute by minute can mix up anyone's head, creating insecurities, building inside like a volcano, ready to erupt. Separation is a double-edged sword. Soldiers can get letters then reinforce their lovers' devotion or get those "dear John" ones prompted by impatience or changes of the heart.

I, being the practical one, knew you wanted to finish your degree and get settled before we embarked on the official marriage journey. I was willing to wait for the formalities, but with life being so precarious, I can understand how you wanted something concrete to hold on to. I agree that the words, boyfriend and girlfriend, were not a sufficient reference to our relationship. They also implied a precariousness without a solid timeframe or commitment.

Judging from my parents and close relative's marriages, I knew that 24/7 togetherness was an unrealistic goal. That "*I do*" is a loaded exclamation. We never really know what we are agreeing to. Life is mysterious that way. Some days there's a lot of "*I don'ts.*"

How did I respond to you? Most likely I reassured you that without any doubt I wanted to marry you and was waiting, fiercely loyal to you and our commitment. I would have asked you what prompted your ardent request. What prompted the impatience? I'm sure the back story would have unraveled and we would have come to a workable conclusion that we both felt comfortable with. I did find a jade band in a little shop nearby which I sent to you to reconfirm our commitment.

I really wasn't as focused as you on the whole wedding day scenario. I never daydreamed about wedding gowns, picking out linens, house wares and the whole hoopla that went into planning a wedding. I would have enjoyed a destination wedding or an informal party. Actually, I was more excited about the honeymoon we planned in Hawaii. I just wanted to be with you, grow together and keep choosing to love you even when there would be obstacles to overcome. I've never been casual about love. It infiltrates me wholly.

When I married Bill, several years after you died, I still didn't have the "bride gene." That came from another fix up with a lot of energy from family and friends to get back out there, whatever that meant. Not being a huntress with men, dating was a chore. Things would have to come naturally. Possibilities emerged but my interest quickly waned. I faked a lot of pleasant smiles.

When Bill came into my life, he knew about you and our story. He was kind, patient and caring. We didn't have the depth that you and I had together. There was always something that made me uneasy. I told myself no one would be exactly like you and not to expect it. So, I allowed my heart to melt.

The secrets he carried came out within a year of marriage. In the middle of this I had a miscarriage. His demons overtook him and the marriage ended within three years. I had no malice towards him. Overall, he had a lot of goodness inside. He truly loved me, but the baggage was too heavy a load to carry. Frankly, I was relieved when it was over. We never saw each other after the divorce.

The losses were mounting inside of me. I immersed myself in my career, travel, creative endeavors and some relationships. I was bruised, but functioning. On the outside, I had it all together, but deep inside I lost my way. You were my guidepost; the one man I trusted to have my back. I wasn't always aware of it, but I was lost without you and somewhere in between I misplaced my soul. It has been a long journey but I'm recovering it, due in part, to re-experiencing our love. The road, once again, leads me back to you.

HAIR

Hi Babe,

Today the engineers killed a cobra snake. I didn't get to see it. They got it on the road outside of the perimeter. It was about 3 feet long. They don't bother anyone as long as you don't bother them. I've seen a few snakes, but I'm not sure what kind they were. They're the least of my worries.

I got a list of colleges from the Dept. of Health, Education and Welfare. They also sent my name to all of them. I'll write to a few. At least now I have some means of communication with the schools. They gave me pre-printed cards. All I have to do is fill in the college name and my return address. That makes things easy.

A barber is here to give haircuts (naturally). I haven't had one since December and that was only a little trim. My ears stay warm when my hair is over them. Everyone kids me about being a hippie and being "back on the block." The CO said if I don't get one this afternoon, he's going to give me one. He was laughing when he said it. I hope he's only kidding! I better rush over and get one.

Love always,
Chip

A few letters later I got the lock of your hair in the mail. When it fell out of letter this time I couldn't believe that after all this time it was still there. A part of you survived! Just feeling its softness brought me back to the way it felt to my touch. I also detected a faint scent when I removed it from the cellophane packet. I put it in a small satin lined box almost the same color as your hair.

When I sent you one of my broken fingernails, you felt the same way about it as I did about your hair. Those small pieces of each other were like gold. It's amazing what hair says about us and the time we inhabited the earth.

The 60's and 70's was about long hair for men and women. I grew mine down to the middle of my back. I was glad you were able to grow it while there. From the news and photos it appeared that they cared less about strict regulations. There was so much more to be concerned about. They could relax over the issue of hair.

The first play I saw as an adult on Broadway was Hair. It was emblematic of the anti-establishment movement. I enjoyed the music. Everyone was dancing in the aisles swaying to the rhythms of peace, love and nakedness! It gave new meaning to live theatre!

My hair was always unruly. It would get frizzy in the summer. I wasn't the only one during that time sleeping with hair wrapped around juice cans (before juice boxes) or ironing it on a higher setting than for the then fashionable polyester clothes we wore.

Long hair, flower power, mini-skirts, bell bottoms and platform shoes were some of the defining factors of our generation. Some things are best left behind, but I'm glad I still have a piece of your unregulated hair.

QUESTIONS

Hi Babe,

I love you! We got in at 9:30 this morning. We got soaking wet walking through the swamps. I stepped into an underwater stream up to my belly button. I couldn't tell because we were in knee deep water already so it couldn't be seen. It was funny because I got stuck in the mud on the bottom and I was helpless. They had to pull me out. I wish I could have gotten a picture for you but it was dark.

I got a lot of mail when I got in. Five letters were from you. I'll try to answer all your questions. The barracks here are real dumpy. There are holes in the floor and in the walls. But after a few nights sleeping with rain, bugs and snakes, anything looks mighty pretty if it has a bed and a roof. There isn't much room, but enough to get to and from the doors. There are about 24 guys in here with double bunks.

Bunker guard is guard of the whole camp. We have a perimeter of bunkers and rolls of wire to keep out the enemy. They try to sneak in and blow up helicopters and other things. So, we set up bunkers with machine guns and M-16's, keeping watch for anyone coming through the wire.

I guess I get enough food. The field is bad for food, but it's enough to get by. We get milk in the mess hall with our meals. It's terrible milk. They call it "filled milk." Money is no problem here. It means nothing. There's not much need for it. The basic necessities they either give us or we can borrow it. The only cost is for snacks and beer.

The people here (Vietnamese) are OK. They mostly keep to themselves. They're not allowed on base unless someone picks them up outside the gate and signs a record for them. They cannot stay after 4:30 p.m. Some guys sign them in to clean up and do their wash. They do good work; there are no favors. They like and need GI money.

I guess that answers all of your questions. I tried to get them all. If you want to know anything, just write it in a letter and I'll let you know. Keep the letters coming! I've been getting a lot from you. It's good to hear from you. I hope you are getting mine. Guess they are coming in spurts from me because I'm in and out a lot. I try to write as much as possible.

I miss you so much. You are always in my thoughts and

dreams. I wish you were in my arms. It would be much better that way. Well, it's time to close. I love you, beautiful!
   Love Always,
   Chip

. . .

I've been curious and inquisitive as far back as I can remember. I think my first words were who, what, where and when. I was always asking questions. My mother once told me a story about how my 2-year old self picked up the phone and the operator (that's when there were telephone operators instead of recordings) came on and I had a full conversation, asking her a bunch of questions. I think I got her life story within five minutes.

I like questions because when you listen to the answers there is a lot to learn. When I listen my mind draws pictures and my senses kick in. I found out that I'm a kinesthetic thinker. For a long time I thought there was something wrong with my thinking, only to find out from an encounter with a business consultant that it was, in fact, an asset. It has served me well, particularly in my work.

It also may explain why I relish thoughtful, forthright investigative journalism. I was thrilled when I got to meet one of my idols, Barbara Walters, when I was in the audience of the TV show, The View, before she retired. I never missed one of her prime time specials.

During one of the commercial breaks, she came out into the audience and I had the opportunity to shake her hand and tell her what her success meant to me. She embraced me! That was a real moment in my life. Her determination, grace, intellectual capacity and ground-breaking achievements for all women gained my lifelong respect and admiration.

I was interested in the details so I could understand what life was like for you. When I read your letters I would picture you wherever you were, doing what you were doing, and somehow I would put myself in your place. I'm glad there's a lapse in time when writing letters. It puts things in perspective. Had I known about some of your experiences immediately I would have been on high alert all the time. Experiencing a bit of your life from far away brings me back to your story about being stuck in the mud.

We want to believe we are so strong and independent until we falter and get stuck in life's experiences. I'm certainly the independent one but over the years I have stepped in things deeper than I could handle alone and felt helpless. Sometimes there are actual arms that lift us and sometimes it's a key learning or understanding that comes from working through the difficulty that eventually lifts us out of the quandary and maybe, as time goes by, we can even laugh at the event that almost brought us under. You were grateful, and so was I, that there were arms, if not mine, to help you.

RAINDROPS

Hi Hon,

I miss you something awful. It's such an empty feeling. It's like I'm only half here. I cannot leave your side. Half of me remained with you to try to keep you from getting down and lonely.

I'm glad you went to see the movie, "Butch Cassidy and the Sundance Kid." It was real wild. Wasn't it? I enjoyed seeing it when I was away before I came home. It reminded me so much of you. That's why I like the Raindrops song. It spells out everything to me. I really don't care about anything that happens here. All I want is for time to pass. My whole attitude now is "big deal—it doesn't mean anything." The only thing that bothers me is being away from you.

I have to answer a lot of letters from everyone, but I'm not in the mood. I enjoy writing to you. When I write I can feel you near me. I just sit back and recall all the times we shared, running around and having so much fun. I look forward to again sharing our time together. I don't know about you, but I enjoy doing anything as long as we are together.

My lips are hurting from a lack of your lips. I already forgot how to kiss. I remember what they're like, though. They're like peanuts or potato chips; once you have one, you just can't stop! All I think about is how much I love you. It makes a lot of memories come alive and I can feel your love come to me. Sometimes, it hurts a little more thinking about it, but it's worth it. I will never stop loving you.

Love Always,
Chip

Before you, I used to avoid the rain. It had to do mostly with the hair. But, we got caught in the rain without an umbrella several times. Somehow it didn't matter how I looked soaking wet. You would just scoop me up in your arms, wipe away the raindrops from my face and tell me how beautiful I looked. I appreciated the little lie.

Back then, a hit movie would play for quite a while. That was before megaplex movie theatres. I still love being transported by a good movie. Even with all the TV movie choices I still love going to the theatre for the full experience of watching a movie. You were always singing that Raindrops song when you were on leave so I was happy I got to see the movie after you left. I still hum that song from time to time. It's now on my phone for easy accompaniment.

I've come to appreciate rainy days. They put me in the right mood for a good book, working on a creative project, or taking an afternoon nap. It's as if the rain gives me permission to relax into the alone time only sharing it with the quiet patter of the raindrops in the background. Rain clears the air and my mental state. During a nap I can see you peddling a bicycle with me singing that song and smelling the clean air after a rainfall. Don't you just love daydreaming?

FAMILY

Hi Babe,

I got three packages yesterday; one was from you, one from my aunt and uncle and one your mom and dad, my in-laws! I really liked your mother's brownies and the other things were great. That salami went fast. Everything she sent was delicious. I haven't eaten it all, but I will.

Hey, Babe, was the ring you were sending me in one of the packages? I looked all over. I even told everyone to eat the brownies in front of me in case you stuck it in one to surprise me. I hope it didn't get lost.

Thanks for everything. I needed the film and books. Thanks for giving me all of your love and happiness. Take care and take all of my love. It's yours. You deserve it and a whole lot more. I hope to be able to give you all you truly deserve—a happy life and family.

I keep thinking of all the wonderful moments we have shared and how much our love has grown and strengthened. I wish we didn't have to have this empty space in between our love. How's the smile coming along? Is it still there? When I am again in your arms we'll both have a reason to show our dimples! Hang in there. I'm coming straight to you—non-stop!

Love eternally,
Chip

Leave it to my mother to send the salami and other edibles. As you got to know, an Italian family is all about the food. No matter what happens in life, the question is always, "*did you eat?*" Food equals love. Every birthday, anniversary and holiday was a cause for celebration governed by several courses of food. We were far from rich but there was always abundant food on the table.

I got a good chuckle from the movie, *Moonstruck*. We could have put my family right into some of those family scenes. Everything was discussed at the dining room table, usually with as many family members as possible. It was annoying back then, but now I sometimes miss that big, boisterous family, especially during the holidays which included endless preparation, cooking, baking and gifts. Things are much smaller and quieter now.

You assimilated quite nicely with their kidding and feeding. That first Christmas your eyes and belly were bulging at the amount of food prepared and eaten. My mother adored you, not withstanding your love for her food. She loved sending those packages to you and the letters always with a bunch of jokes. She loved to make you laugh. It didn't take much. You were always a good sport.

Both of my parents readily welcomed you into the family and considered you their son-in-law, especially when you were deployed. It was never that easy for anyone else after you. I didn't realize it at the time how much my entire extended family was also affected when you didn't return home. I was so numb that I couldn't have noticed, but in retrospect, appreciated that they were there for me in their own way, especially my aunts and uncles.

My relationship with my mother wasn't an easy one. Her driving need for perfection kept me on edge for most of my childhood years. Sometimes she was very hard on me and other times she was the generous giver of gifts. I had to be prepared for whatever side showed up which created a lot of inner tension. My father remained on the sidelines most of the time.

After my mother died, quite young, my father and I became closer. He lived to 97. With years and some wisdom I now understand their motivations much better. I try to think of my mother through my "belly button" theory: when I look down at my naval, it is a reminder that whatever the circumstances afterwards, she gave me space to grow, launching me out into the life I have. I can then extract the love from the emotional ancestral baggage we all carry.

Your parents treated me like a daughter. They included me in everything when you were away. I loved spending time at your house. I always felt warm, welcomed and relaxed when I was in their presence. Of course, a lot of the fun was around the fire department activities. We shared your photos, packages, letters (the un-sexy ones) while you were away. I will always be grateful for their kindness, love and inclusion which extended beyond your death.

Even though you had an Italian last name, it was an adopted name, so my family antics were fun to you. I would roll my eyes, but your baby blue eyes would twinkle. You thought it was all so exotic. I wanted to run away at times and change my last name to Simpson or Smith!

It's interesting how we identify with family names and identities. But, I've come to know that a lot of it comes from the family we inherited. A few years ago, I decided to get my DNA tested. It turns out that my ethnicity only has about 8% Italian in it. My blood line is mostly Greek, Middle Eastern and North African. So, it begs the question—are we who we think we are? It's was a curious twist for me and it got me thinking. If we take away the borders, flags, religious institutions and peel back our skin, aren't we are all just human beings

THE EXCHANGE

Hi Love,

I'm listening to the tape you sent. It sure is good hearing your voice again. It's no nice hearing "I love you" right from you. You sounded depressed. Cheer up. Life's not that bad. That's one thing

you learn over here because it can end so fast. I'm not saying it to scare you. It's a fact that comes alive here.

I also got two letters from you today with some more questions for me to answer. I'll answer them straightforwardly, but don't start worrying. Deal?

I'm neutral in feelings about this place. In some respects it's ok, but in others it's bad. I haven't spent much money. That's good news because when I get back I'll have lots of savings. The bad news is that there are lots of the V.C. in the area. We've gotten sniper fire from the village and the whole area is heavily booby trapped.

On my birthday one of my friends tripped one and he's now on his way to Japan. He took a lot of shrapnel in his legs and left arm. He will be ok. It's just one of those things. It can't be helped. A lot of villagers come here with shrapnel in them after they have hit one.

I sleep on the ground here in the village. They have little cubby hole bunkers, but I only sleep in them if it looks like rain. There are rats in all of them. It's not as bad as it sounds.

You asked about how I feel about fighting. That's a funny question. It's not too bad if everyone works together. I get a real good feeling inside when things go well. I don't feel scared until after we stop firing. Then I think of what could have happened. After an ambush we have to sweep the area and check for bodies. That's scary because it's dark and they could be lying there waiting. We count the bodies and check them. We take everything from them except their clothes. Anything that looks important, Intelligence will check out.

The first time I saw a dead V.C. I felt funny but you get used to it. It's all a "him or me" deal. Once that's straight in your head, you realize how you have to act.

The radio is just a box on my back. All I do is set a few dials and then push a button on the receiver and talk. It's battery run. I learned that in training. The rest I just picked up along the way, like fixing parts.

> We never get days off. Every day is the same. Saigon is off limits for the 25th Infantry because a few guys shot up the place long ago. Most of the time guys talk about our patrols and what we were doing in the field. It's good to discuss different ideas for future use. Usually after mail call everyone talks about home and what is happening there.
> I must go now. Take care and keep up that smile! I love you.
> Love forever,
> Chip

. . .

How can I imagine what it is like to kill another human? I know you were trained to protect yourself and your fellow soldiers. But, what is it like to see a body without life at the other end of your rifle, to remove it and the person's belongings? War does strange things to humans. It's as old as time.

In real life, most of us couldn't bear the thought of this, but only the soldier knows what it's like to walk in his or her boots and to have to take a life in exchange for your own. Aren't the victims on both ends? What about the civilians that are always caught up in the middle of the carnage?

This isn't a judgment call; just the desire to know what was really going through your mind. I would never know. If you had returned and done this for seven more months would it have been classified in your mind as a bad dream or would you have carried the images and the wounds home with you?

When I watch documentaries, movies or read stories about war, my first thoughts are usually about the soldier's psyche and the price that is paid for the exchange. I think that is why most soldiers do not want to talk about it when they get home. They need to assimilate into what you called the "real world" and those thoughts get pushed as far back as they will go. I understand this because for a very long time I would not talk about what I witnessed on 9/11. I would only speak about it with one person who was with me on that day and we usually don't get into details.

I would like to think that because of the kind of "no secrets' agreement we made early on, that at some point, probably lying under a tree or someplace in the soothing aspects of nature, you would have gradually revealed that part of your life. I also know with certainty that you kept those deeper details inside yourself to protect me from fear. No one can do that but it was a gallant gesture. I am a lot stronger than I thought I was. Time has taught me that.

I only know this. If I had the same training as you had, I would approach it as my duty, as you did. I would try to separate a part of my mind to place the images so I could go on. I also know that whatever ghosts you brought home I would make friends with them because I knew your true heart and there wasn't anything I wouldn't do to ease your pain. We were each other's safe haven for the truth.

I had no illusions about the realities of life and war, but I was willing to take the bet and roll the dice with you. You were so worth it.

LOVE & LIKE

Hi Babe,

Today there's a real nice breeze blowing. It's sunny and not too hot. It's a perfect day. It would be a nice day to spend together.

I wish I knew what to say. The words can't describe how I feel. You're everything to me. Its' like you and I are the only two people in the world. Whatever I do I think of how my actions will affect you and whatever happens to me, I always think of how you will feel. Everything works off of our love. Without that beautiful love we share, I'd be lifeless.

With you I can really live and be myself. Without you, I could only exist. I'm glad we have such a strong love. If I didn't have your love I could never feel all this happiness and these feelings. Right now everything is based on memories and the love that could never leave or be forgotten.

We have to live like this for another 10 months. It sure is hard to live this way and suppress these loving feelings. When we are together and don't have to suppress them, we will release all of ourselves to each other and makes room for our love to grow even more. Now, I can only experience this love through letters and dreams.

I can feel our love exchanging with each letter. I never would have believed what love can do if I had not met you. When I'm home we will make all this misery go away. We will again do all the things we like doing together.

Take good care of yourself. I'll be making love with you in my dreams. I know you will be doing the same. Somehow, we always know when we are thinking of each other.

I will love you always,
Chip

. . .

I have come to realize that love and like are two different things. We can be in love with the idea of love and get disappointed by reality. We can feel love because we are excited to be around the other person. Over time, we may find through actions that we may not really like how the person behaves in situations, especially challenging ones. Love, sometimes, is just not enough, to complete a journey together. That's where "like" comes in.

My measurement is if you can handle the everyday life experiences together, be your authentic self, and actually enjoy the other's company most of the time, then you've gotten the winning ticket. Love grows easier when you truly like the person you are with and how you feel about yourself when you are with them. There aren't any loose ends lurking in the background.

We had that auspicious combination. I do not remember a

single cringe worthy situation where I thought, *"what was I thinking?"* Subsequent to you, I've had that thought on several occasions. Whenever I was in your presence, I felt like a plant given the perfect amount of light, soil and water to grow and flourish.

You were the first person to like me for the emerging person I was without expectation. I didn't have to do anything to earn your love. It was a given and I reciprocated in kind. It was a wonderful experience to truly love another person without question, to give unselfishly, to shed inhibitions and to tell the truth. I was one lucky gal to have that opportunity with you.

When I placed my head on your chest I felt relaxed and at peace. I would exhale. When I felt your heartbeat, mine matched yours. No matter what was happening outside of our nest, I was safe and loved. There was no need to be on high alert. We were far from perfect but we were perfectly aligned together. In fact, the imperfections we discovered in each other strengthened our relationship. We were attentive to each other's needs and were comfortable seeing where the unscripted road would take us.

Our letters continued to uncover the nuances of each other's hearts and minds. They weren't just words strung together. They were a fortification that gave connectivity and balance to each other. It was an intricate dance but one that moved seamlessly. I understood your sense of completeness when we were together. It has taken me so many years to feel complete with myself without you. Yet, underneath it all, I believe in some way, you have continued to nourish and encourage my growth. Maybe that completeness escaped death.

VOICES

Hi Love,

How is everything with you? I love you! Yesterday I got the package with the ring! It's really beautiful! Now I officially feel married to you. Please get one to match. I will send you the money.

I love the new medal and peace sign replacing the ones I lost. I'll enjoy the book. I am going to bring it out with me today while on guard duty.

I finally got my tape recorder. I made a tape for you last night. You should get it shortly. I'll make another in the near future.

I enjoyed the tapes you made for me with all the music. As I wrote you, my radio got stolen so this is the only good music I can listen to, so I appreciate it very much. You take such good care of me. I now notice how much you lift my spirits. You are everything and more to me.

I have to say goodbye for now. Take care, my love, Smile! I'm all yours!

Love Ya!

Chip

The 90-minute tape came in late February. It was the first time I heard your voice since you left in December. I can't fully explain how that felt. All of our memories spilled into my ears through your voice. I could feel what it was like to be near you.

When I found the tape in the suitcase I immediately played it. I sobbed for hours. That familiar voice was still alive. Half way through it, the tape broke. I wept even more loudly. Within a few days, I finally located a media specialist who could repair the tape. The stars aligned and within three weeks, I had the repaired tape, a CD and a flash drive with your voice. I am still amazed how this magic occurred. The new technology made your voice even clearer.

It had a mixture of background noises of chopper engines, grenade launchers, star clusters and other military sounds that you explained as they occurred. After that, when the excitement died down, it was all about the love we shared and how much I meant to you.

You spoke on a Friday night under a full moon beneath a tree while back on base in Tay Ninh after spending several weeks in a village. It was exactly one month before you departed. You spoke about your next assignment that was to be near Saigon and how you didn't regret having this big experience, except for the distance between us. This was consistent with your letters. You made peace with it. This was your "government job" for the time being.

While you were speaking, medivacs were coming in. That sound of the whirling helicopter blades will always haunt me. Also, a CS grenade went off which propelled a high level of gas near the perimeter from where you were speaking. Your eyes and nose were burning and it affected your breathing. What else had you been exposed to that would have affected your well being?

The rest of it focused on us. You told me how good it felt to know you were loved by me and how I was your inspiration and couldn't do what you had to do without me in your life. You always felt me near, especially when you were scared. You knew everything would be ok. You never worried about our love fading; it was there from the beginning and would last forever. You recalled so many memories that had kept you going.

You ended with some sweet music. Your last words were *"want to dance?"* Oh, how I wish that was possible, but I was satisfied that I could at least continue to hear you and fantasize about the dance.

I was so happy that you put on that jade band and it was with you until the end. I never did get to obtain a matching ring for myself. I found an infinity ring in a shop recently that is on my ring finger of my left hand. It is a symbol of our eternal love. I know you would have liked that.

LITTLE THINGS

Good morning Hon,

Wow! I got three letters today. I didn't expect any mail today because I got two yesterday from you. I had another thing that surprised me. I'm staying in tonight. No patrol. That's fantastic! I can stay in and write by candlelight to you. Sound good?

Things like that really make a day. I even got extra chicken for supper. I've learned to appreciate the little things. It makes me sort of happy when things go like that. Usually everything here is the same old crap and just a hard time. Today it was worth it. I even got your pictures from the holidays! You look so great in them. You're really beautiful. I just want to jump into the picture and jump into your arms.

How is everything with you? I know school work is getting harder and may not be so easy to write. Don't worry, Barb. Just write when you have enough time. No matter how long it is between letters, always remember that somewhere I'm saying how much I love you. That's always tops in my mind.

I've been able to save most of my pay for us. I'll be getting a raise and that will help me save for a car to be paid off before we get married. Remember those things I was thinking about, but never told you? Well, here goes. Do you want to get engaged on your birthday in August?

Sorry, I spoiled the surprise but I want to know. I've been thinking about it for a while. This way when I return we can have our plans in place in advance. We'll have enough to have the party and I'm sure we can have the firehouse for it, unless something goes wrong before I get home. Sorry. I'm always thinking of that too. Let me know how you feel about this. OK?

Barb, I miss your touch, your lips on mine and the closeness *we share. But, most of all I miss just doing those everyday little things together. When we talk about something it really means so much to both of us. I miss not talking things through with you. It's hard to write about these things, especially about our love and plans. You probably realize that also.*

Sometimes I feel so lonely without you. Not only are we lovers but no one could come close to being such a good friend as you are to me. We can talk about anything with each other. You're my best friend. I love you so very much.

Well, it's time to go. Soon we'll be together again. That will be our day! Keep on giving me all of that beautiful love. I'm all yours. Come take all my love. I want to give it all to you.

Love Forever,
Chip

. . .

You were so right about the little things in life. When I think back it wasn't a particular major event we shared. It was those small gestures, unplanned surprises and everyday things we did together that resonated the most with me. It was the ease between us that made the smallest of things so special. Being both in college, we had limited funds, but we made the most of every experience together. We felt rich just winning the jackpot with each other.

I still appreciate the little things. Last night there was an amazing sunset and I thought how we would be just as happy taking a short ride to the beach to watch it as we would from a luxurious vacation spot. Appreciation is a gift. The more time I spend on the planet I realize how little I need to be happy. I do enjoy the big adventures but my heart sings just as much with a good book, fresh air and a meaningful conversation.

Being physically apart heightened that awareness. The excitement every time a letter from you landed in the mailbox was a cause for celebration. The sound of your voice on that tape brought me to tears. I think most of life is a series of big and little steps. While the big steps get one going faster, it's the little steps that make one pause and appreciate all the bones and muscles in the feet that make it possible.

You made love possible for me with the simplest of words and gestures. It's the little things you did and said that are forever imprinted in my heart. Being reminded of this makes it a good day for me too.

PLANS

Hi Doll,

I'm leaving in two hours for patrol tonight. We're supposed to be in again before noon tomorrow. It's going to be another wet one. We're going by riverboat. That means we stomp through the rice paddies and swamps again.

You wouldn't believe how tired I am. I feel like I am going to pass out. My eyes are half closed already. t's going to be hassle keeping awake for guard duty.

I'm reading the book you sent. I really like it so far. I've read about half of it already. I can always use books. I like reading when I have free time so I can to learn something new about life. Thanks for sending it. That crossword book is something else. I'm learning new words! I think my knowledge is too narrow and I want to keep learning new things.

We had a few incoming rockets about two hours ago. They landed pretty close, not in my specific area, but enough to drive us to the floor and under bunks. It's nothing to worry about.

"When I Die" by Blood, Sweat & Tears is on the radio. Memories!!! Our child will be the one to carry on. Maybe there will also be brothers and sisters!

I have a request. Will you tape up some more albums for me? Sounds from home are best because I know your love is with each and every song. We've heard our music so many times together and it will bring a bit of our happiness over here.

I really don't know what I would do here without your love and help. You really make things a lot better, especially all the letters and packages. I could never express my appreciation for all your support. It's a great feeling having you loving and pushing for me. I wish there was something I could do for you in return. If there's anything you need or want, don't hesitate to ask. I'll get whatever I can here. Don't be afraid to try me!

I can't wait for that day to come when we are together again. It's on its way already. As long as things keep steady we'll soon be forgetting this year and starting on our uninterrupted future. Before you know it, we'll be planning our wedding, then our family and then our children's futures. It's going to be sneaking up on us, so we better start getting prepared. There's a lot we can start discussing and making plans for. I want the best for us.

I don't mind telling anyone that you are going to be my wife and that you are the most beautiful woman I've ever seen. I'm so much in love with you. You are the greatest!

Love Eternally,
Chip

. . .

It still pains me to think how close we got to making our plans a reality. I think plans make things seem attainable. They are concrete constructs that we can relate to. I am now ambivalent about plans. I like the basic knowledge and details when planning a dinner or a trip but I don't want to know the outcome. I want to limit chaos but leave some things to chance. Maybe I no longer trust those "best laid plans." Life marches to its own beat.

I am constantly reminded that so much of life is out of my control. The illusion of control is enticing but unrealistic. I keep having to learn this lesson. Life determines the outcome. I certainly had no control over our future or the one we believed we had.

There are many tomes that state the opposite view; that we make our own destiny. When I look back I've said yes or no to things that put me on different paths, but I'm not so sure whether another choice would have changed my life so dramatically. It is one of those questions that does not have a distinct answer. I think we get what we get and it's our choice how we play the game of life. We make millions of choices that can lead us to our destination.

I choose to believe that you and I were part of each other's destiny, even for the short earthly time we had together. After you, I had to rebuild my life singularly. I'll never want to label it "good" or "bad" but uncertainty followed me around like a puppy. I have developed a newfound appreciation for resiliency. It's a required companion for the journey.

HUMOR & TRUST

> Hi Love,
>
> Just a few lines before I go out on patrol. I must tell you "I love you" before I go. Want to come out with me tonight? You can set up with me and pull guard duty. It gets lonely sitting alone. You can sleep with me in my poncho liner. I'm sure we can fit if we snuggle up real close.
>
> I hear that we're moving from Tay Ninh. I hope not. Tay Ninh is a good area of operation for us. If we leave, that will mean that we will have to work in different areas than we are now. Our areas aren't too bad. There are a lot worse in the 25th Infantry's area. Only time will tell. It's still in the rumor stage.
>
> Barb, I need you to know I'll always be true to you. I could never do you wrong. You're too much a part of me. I know I can confide in you and get your help, no matter what. You mean everything to me. Our minds act as one and our lives are based on

being one. Soon we will be sharing our lives as husband and wife. I can't wait till that day comes. I want to be able to work for our home and family. I always look forward to making you happy and pleasing you. You know how I feel.

Hey, please don't worry about me. I'm doing fine. I'm not going crazy. I'm keeping my cool. I don't do anything stupid. I'm far from gung-ho. All I do is what I'm supposed to or whatever I can without getting hurt.

Well, time to go now. Take care and don't worry. See you soon!

Forever yours,

Chip

I'm trying to picture myself pulling guard duty with you squeezed into a poncho liner under the night sky. If it wasn't war time, it would be very funny. We would probably argue over who had more room and you would tickle me till I burst out into uncontrollable laughter. You knew all my ticklish spots.

I could never stay mad at you for more than a few minutes. You always had a way of working your way back into my heart. You never had a problem saying you were sorry, which is a great advantage in a relationship and marriage! Of course, I'd annoy you sometimes when I overanalyzed something and you just wanted to get on with it.

It worked because even though we were serious about each other, we didn't take ourselves too seriously. No subject was taboo. You never had trouble asking questions about me and listened thoughtfully to my answers. I didn't have to take precautionary measures. I felt lighter around you. I think you trusted me because I told the truth. I could ask you anything and you reciprocated with the same honesty. We refrained from judgment.

Because we both wanted the same things in life, a balance between roots and adventure, we probably would have grown through the years like any seasoned couple, moving to the rhythm of the inevitable ups and downs, pleasures and disagreements but with an inner smile of knowing that we would get through it together.

Humor and trust were the winning combination. We were building a solid foundation.

CARDS

Hi Barb,

Today we worked on our new position for tonight. It's pretty nice. We have sand bags in the front and put poncho liners over the top for shade. We put a strand of Constantine wire around the whole area.

It's almost time to eat. I think I smelled chicken before. I hope so. I'm really hungry. It's getting towards sunset. It's cooling down a bit. That's good. I wish we were together now. We could sit and watch the sun go down together.

I don't know what else to say. I guess "I love you" are my only words. That should be my only vocabulary because those words are always on my mind. I constantly relate everything I do, as us doing it together. In my mind we could accomplish anything. I always think of all the fun we had doing things together, even chores! I want that all back.

I'm sending a few cards I have here. I won't be needing them. You can hang on to them. I like to send you things of mine; that's all I have for now. One is my 25th combat card, just showing I've been in combat and I'm in the 25th Infantry. The other is my Geneva Convention card. That is so if I ever become a prisoner, they will treat me well. It wouldn't help any even if I'm ever captured. I won't need it because I know I'll never get caught. It's just something for you to look at because it's part of me.

Well, have to go. Take care. You're the greatest! Smile, I love you.

Love eternally,
Chip

. . .

We were always sending each other cards, even when you were back home. I found some with the letters in the suitcase. The ones I liked best from you were the handmade ones. You would make them from discarded cardboard or anything you got your hands on and drew pictures and wrote funny or sentimental sayings. Those are so precious, like the ones children make for their parents which are hung on refrigerator doors. They bring a smile to my face because of the personal effort. Hallmark had nothing on you.

Now, the other cards were a different story. I also found those. The combat one states: "This is to certify that you, having served in combat with the 25th Infantry Division is a member in good standing of the Tropic Lightning Association."

The Geneva Convention card merely states that it was issued to you by the Armed Forces of the United States in accordance with the provisions of the Geneva Convention of August 12, 1949. It also says, "Property of the United States Government–If Found, Drop in Nearest U.S. Mail Box." A lot of good that would do you back home. Both are in perfect condition as if they were issued today.

I'm not sure why those disturbed me so much. My first thought was why you didn't keep them with you. Would they make a difference if something happened to you? I was also struck by your confidence about not getting captured. Maybe that was youth's bravado talking. Or maybe, there was something else fate was trying to tell me.

I've wracked my brain as to why I was so perplexed by those cards. I've come up empty. In the end, you didn't need either one of them. Sometimes a card is just a card.

ON THE MOVE

Hi Barb,

I love you! I was only out one night in two days. We were called in for support on Black Virgin Mountain. It was a real bummer climbing it. We only went a little ways up. It was all rocks and caves. We found a few grenades and some ammo. Luckily we didn't see any V.C.

We were called in because a recon platoon took heavy casualties—2 killed and 5 wounded in action. The enemy was nowhere to be seen. They took off into the caves to hide. Going on that mountain is like going into North Vietnam or Cambodia. I'm mighty glad we got through it.

In two days we leave Tay Ninh for good. We're moving to Fire Station Base Rhode Island. (I would have liked to hear "Long Island!") It's near the Saigon area. I think it will be hard, but not as dangerous. I'll let you know.

You make me so very happy. I could never go on without you. You know, not that I'm thinking anything bad, but if anything ever happened to come between us, I would just stay here. I'd rather live like this than not have you. I would re-enlist and remain in Nam indefinitely. That's how much you mean to me. I will love you forever and ever and ever.

Well, tonight is an early night. I'll have to pack up. Take good care of yourself. Goodnight, my love.

Yours and Only Yours,
Chip

It seemed to me that you were always on the move. The patrols were almost every night and the days were for building, taking down and preparing to move. You were in swamps, rice paddies and dense wooded areas. You had no say in the matter. Orders had to be fulfilled. You were off to a new base within a short time. I now had another location to circle on the map.

Black Virgin Mountain was in the news quite frequently due to the high level of military action and its voluminous caves, which created a hostile environment for combat. Its close proximity to Cambodia and to the North Vietnamese supply chain, the Ho Chi Minh trail, made it particularly challenging and took its share of casualties over the course of the war. I was always on edge when the mountain made the news.

What made it more compelling is the myth about the mountain that involved love, betrayal and death, which held significance for the population. It is now a tourist attraction, like many other parts of Vietnam, and is a historical site with a temple. I wonder how much has been revealed about the casualties on both sides to maintain the mountain and its myth.

In any war, there are always iconic physical reminders of mountains, bridges, walls, hills, rivers and beaches that leave an indelible mark on the memories of a war. Books and movies are created about the events surrounding these monuments, but the personal stories are the most poignant. That is why, I believe, letters are so powerful. It bears the truth directly from the individual's thoughts and recollections.

Now you were off to a new base, which was further away from the mountain. It brought me little relief. What challenges would that new assignment bring?

TIMING

Hi Love,

How is everything with you? I'm completely moved out of Tay Ninh now. We are down between Saigon and Bien Hoa. I made a mark on the little map below to show you our approximate location. It's a lot different from our other area of operation. There aren't any rice paddies. It's all thick woods and jungle and not easy to travel through. But, there are no booby traps and it is much safer. Now, all I have to worry about are snakes and scorpions!

I haven't seen our Fire Support base yet. We came straight from Tay Ninh to the jungles. I won't get into base for another few days. We'll be going out on night patrols before settling in on the base.

The Manchu's will be leaving Vietnam soon. They are going to Alaska. That will be quite a climate change. I wouldn't mind adjusting to the cold. A few guys will be going, but naturally not me. I guess we'll get sent to different battalions in the 25th division. Maybe I'll get to go home early if the entire 25th division moves out of here in about six or seven months.

I never got to send that package to you. I'll try to send it to you in about 40 days. I know it's a long wait but that's the best I can do. I think I may be able to call you, but I won't be able to write and estimate a date because it will just happen. I'll try to make it very late here so I can reach you. Everything here is very unorganized. I just want you to know that the first chance I get, I will definitely call you.

I'm working on getting you our engagement and wedding rings. We can get them from a military connected mail jeweler. I wrote away for the catalogue. I'll see if there is anything nice. It will take a while. In the meantime, please send me your ring size.

I'm really going to lose a lot of weight now. All we get to eat are C-rations. We get one hot meal every six days; the rest are C-rations. I have to live out of my rucksack until we finish out the next 60-90 days.

Well, Babe, I must go now. Take care of yourself. I love you.
Forever yours,
Chip

. . .

So close, yet so far away. If we had more time, I would have had more letters and would have spoken to you from the other side of the planet. I would have received the package and our rings. You may have gotten to leave there and go to Alaska and I could have travelled to see you before you came home for good. But, timing was not on our side.

Time feels so different when we are waiting for something as opposed to looking back or focused on the present. When events interrupt a relationship we are either looking back on memories or planning a future to sustain us while we are in different time zones.

When I received this letter I didn't know how precarious time would be. I could only be patient and relish every word you wrote while running my fingers over the map to try to move with you through the woods and jungles.

I wish I could have stopped time and prevented the inevitable. I thought my will would protect you from any harm. Love does funny things to a person. Destiny has its own timeline.

IN THE JUNGLE

Hi Babe,

Last night I kept waking up and thinking of you. I kept reaching out to take you in my arms. I felt so lonely. This morning when I woke up I started thinking of how much I miss you. When I thought of the nine months till we would be together, tears came to my eyes. I really don't know how I'll be able to last nine months without you. I guess when I get a letter, I'll feel better. Maybe today I'll get one. I really feel down. Sorry for writing like this.

Everything here is still messed up. The changing of plans makes everything more difficult. They never brought out clean clothes for us. I've had the same stuff on for five days already. You can imagine how they look and smell! I should have had a picture taken this morning before I shaved. I looked in the mirror and I didn't believe it was me. The shave helped out a little. They just brought out water so I'll be able to take a shower later. We are located in a clearing with red, dusty dirt. Everything gets filthy in a matter of minutes.

I'm sitting in a rubber plantation. I tapped my first rubber tree. It was real cool. White stuff oozes out from the bark and in about 30 minutes the white stuff hardens into rubber. It looks like rubber bands. That's it for the excitement here.

I'm getting thirsty and I'm almost out of water. I only carried two quarts with me this time. I was carrying three quarts but a friend of mine had only one canteen, so I gave him one of mine. He wouldn't have lasted very long with only one quart. When you start walking here in the jungle, you sweat like rain.

Later, I'll look for a stream or some bamboo trees. They are filled with water and good to drink. Every joint in bamboo is filled with water when it's growing and still green. All you do is cut a hole in the bottom of a joint and hold a canteen or a cup there. It just drips out. Then you cut another hole on top of the joint and it all flows out. One tree will give out a lot of water if you get every joint.

It's almost time for lunch. I'll fix you lunch if you want to eat with me. Today we'll have a big lunch (I brought a lot of extra food for us). Let's take a look and see what we feel like having. Well, there's boned turkey in broth, crackers and peanut butter, peaches, hot chocolate and two ounces of pound cake with some chocolate to dip it in, so it doesn't taste so dry. That's a pretty big lunch for here. It's better than a C-ration lunch with only meat, fruit and crackers.

I love you! Why don't you wrap yourself up in a big package and send yourself over to me? You could put food and water in it. Then, when you get here, I'll get in it with you and we can send ourselves to another country. This way we can be together! When I get home, let's do all of our traveling together. If you and I want to go someplace, let's go to those "someplaces" together.

Well, I have to shower and get ready to leave. Take care. Stay mine forever and ever! I'm all yours and only yours, so you're stuck with me!

I love you,
Chip

. . .

I was already interested by the descriptions of your daily life. How else would I understand what living in a jungle was all about? It wasn't a travel excursion with anecdotal stories given by a guide. It was the real deal with you as my guide. You took me into places I'd never been up to that time, literally and figuratively. If there wasn't a war going on, it would actually be an enjoyable documentary of this new part of the world you were living in.

When my father was in WWII, stationed on Guam, he took a lot of pictures. I still love to pour through them. There was a lot of destruction when he arrived, just having secured the island back from Japan, but there was also so much beauty in the tropical terrain, pristine beaches, graceful trees and especially in the faces of the people. I try to imagine myself there through his camera lens. He didn't focus on the devastation; he depicted its beauty and fortified his love of nature through those pictures.

When you wrote about your surroundings and sent photos, I would join you in my mind and it brought wonder to me, even for a short time, when I could take my mind off of the war and its consequences.

That simple lunch reminded me of our picnics together whenever we spent time in nature. It didn't matter if it was in the woods, a park or a beach. As long as we were together, everything was tasty. We knew how to make a feast out of the basic of things.

REMAINS

Hi Babe,

We are going out for nine days so I figured I'd write before we leave. Don't worry if you don't get much mail when we leave. I'll write each day so when we do come in (or a chopper comes out to pick up the mail), you will get my letters. Sorry about that, but it will be very irregular for the whole time I'm out there.

I want to tell you of the love my heart holds for you. When our lips touch and our arms hold each other, no words are needed to explain our love. A kiss does better than any words I could ever write. Knowing that the love we share is so great and strong, makes things much easier.

Just look out when I return! I'm going to run to you at the airport. It's going to be hard to resist just taking you into my arms. I hope I can hold back my feelings until we are alone! Once we are alone, there will be no holding back for either of us. I will reread all your letters so I will remember all of your wants and desires and I will ease them for you.

Well, I must go. Bye, Bye, Baby. Watch for me in your dreams. I'll be there! I LOVE YOU!!!

Your Husband Forever,
Chip

Those were your last words I received, written to me on March 7, 1970. You went out on a mission and were most likely carrying more letters waiting to be mailed to me when you got back to base. An accident prevented that from happening. The official U.S. government incident report reads as follow:

AT THIRTEEN HUNDRED HOURS, ON 12 MARCH 1970, U.S. ARMY HELICOPTER 66-1207 DEPARTED

PHU LOI AIRFIELD AS CHALK FOUR IN A FLIGHT OF FOUR UH-1'S WITH A DESTINATION OF A PICKUP ZONE AT YS 3880. THE PRIMARY MISSION WAS TO PARTICIPATE IN A TACTICAL EXTRACTION OF SIXY-SEVEN U.S. ARMY INFANTRY TROOPS, AND RETURN THEM TO FSB RHODE ISLAND, IN SUPPORT OF THE 25TH INFANTRY DIVISION. THE FLIGHT TO THE PICKUP ZONE WAS UNEVENTFUL. UPON RECEIVING THE REQUIRED INFORMATION FROM THE AIR MISSION COMMANDER THE FLIGHT LEADER PROCEEDED TOWARD THE PZ. AT THIS TIME THE AMC TOLD THE FLIGHT LEADER TO BE PREPARED TO CARRY EIGHT TO TEN GROUND TROOPS ON EACH OF HIS FOUR AIRCRAFT IN ORDER TO SAVE AN EXTRA TURN AROUND. THE GROUND TROOPS HAD BEEN LINED UP, SEVEN MEN PER AIRCRAFT AND HAD TO SHIFT THEIR PERSONNEL ON THE GROUND IN ORDER TO COMPLY WITH AMC'S INSTRUCTIONS. THE PICKUP ZONE WAS LARGE AND NO PROBLEMS WERE ENCOUNTERED ON THE TAKEOFF BY THE AIRCRAFT IN THE FLIGHT. THE FLIGHT PROCEEDED SOUTHEAST TOWARD THE LANDING ZONE AND CLIMBED TO AN ALTITUDE OF TWO HUNDRED FEET ABOVE THE GROUND. AFTER BEING AIRBORNE APPROXIMATELY THREE MINUTES, AND IN THE VICINITY OF THE ACCIDENT SITE, YS 4077, THE AIRCRAFT COMMANDER OF THE CHALK FOUR AIRCRAFT U.S. ARMY HELICOPTER SERIAL NUMBER 66-1207, WAS HEARD TO SAY OVER THE UHF RADIO "27 HAS AN ENGINE FAILURE, GOING DOWN IN THE TREES." IN AN ATTEMPT TO PREPARE FOR IMPACT WITH THE TREES WO1 CUNNINGHAM INITIATED A SEVERE DECELERATION AT THIS POINT THE TAILBONE HIT A 10 INCH DIAMETER TREE BREAKING IT AND CAUSING THE AIRCRAFT TO

PIVOT ON THE POINT OF CONTACT). AS A RESULT OF THE DECELERATION MANEUVER AND CONTACT WITH THE TREES THE AIR SPEED WAS NEAR ZERO BUT THE PIVOTING ACTION CAUSED THE AIRCRAFT TO ENTER THE TREES IN A NOSE LOW ALTITUDE. UPON IMPACT WITH THE TREES AN INITIAL EXPLOSION OCCURRED AND A FIRE ENSUED. THE AIRCRAFT WAS SEEN FALLING NEARLY VERTICALLY TO THE GROUND IN A BALL OF FLAMES. NUMEROUS SMALLER EXPLOSIONS WERE SEEN ONCE THE AIRCRAFT CAME TO REST ON THE GROUND. APPROXIMATELY TWO TO THREE MINUTES AFTER THE AIRCRAFT HIT THE GROUND A TREMENDOUS EXPLOSION OCCURRED, SENDING DEBRIS FROM THE BURING WRECKAGE SEVERAL HUNDRED FEET IN THE AIR SPREADING THE WRECKAGE OVER A 375 METER DIAMETER CIRCLE.

The night before at approximately the same time, figuring the 12-hour time difference, I awaked from a deep sleep with my heart pounding, difficulty breathing and sweating profusely. It took a while to calm myself, talk myself out of thinking I was having a heart attack and get my breathing under control before returning to a restless sleep. Was it a random dream, a coincidence or a premonition? I'll never know. What I do know is that it felt so real; as if I was there with you. In some way, I probably was because a part of me died with you in that explosion.

    There were no survivors out of the thirteen aboard the aircraft. You were one of nine passengers and four crew members that perished. It was declared a non-hostile accident. During recent further investigation I found out your helicopter was the second one used for the extraction to return to base. The soldiers waiting for the third helicopter witnessed the explosion and had to sign a statement indicating that they witnessed it, attesting to the lack of remains for military and insurance purposes.

Remains. What an inadequate word to explain a physical being. How does one begin to fathom what was carried within that being; all the experiences, people encountered, breaths taken, hopes and dreams, countless thoughts and actions, the heart and soul, the love given and received. What happens to all of that when a body is ripped apart?

It took weeks for the military to declare the death. In between, you were missing in action. What were we to do with that information? Waiting for confirmation all kinds of images came into our heads. Did you escape? Were you a prisoner of war? What do we do when placed in the middle of the possibility of life and the certainty of death? How do you go along with your day existing in the middle?

Hope was the word we used to get through the days and nights which blurred into a dazed dream until the official notice came. Then I sunk to my knees and melted into oblivion.

*"You have to keep breaking your heart
until it opens."*
~Rumi

AFTERMATH

My dear, sweet, loving, fire fighter,

You were saved from a barracks fire and destroyed by a fiery explosion. You could not escape your final encounter with fire. It engulfed your body and all of us that loved you.

It took almost two months for what was left of you to be returned to arrange the funeral and burial. We acted as if in suspended animation, a perpetual state of disbelief, as we waited for the final arrangements. Most of that time was like being in a relentless fog. Movement took incredible effort. I was alive but part of me died with you.

You were posthumously elevated to Corporal rank which offered little consolation to me considering the circumstances. It was an honorable accommodation but a badge that couldn't begin to define you.

Part of the main street in town was closed off for the funeral. So many people lined the streets and filled the funeral home. The volunteer fire department draped the flags over the raised ladders to honor you. It was a very sad day but I don't remember crying. I was still so numb.

I do remember someone coming up to me saying, "at least

you weren't married and have children." It felt like I had taken a bullet to my heart. I will never forget the momentary feeling of rage I felt inside from those words. We WERE wed in so many ways. I made a vow to myself that day that I would only say "I'm sorry for your loss" rather than any inane remark just to fill space.

During the months afterwards, your mother, father and brother, Paul, were the ones who held me up. I would spend as much time around them as possible to still feel your presence surrounding me. It was as if they were holding a piece of you for me. As always, they treated me as part of the family, especially during this tender time with kindness and respect. They included me in the necessary decisions.

We were all grieving in our own way. Your father had a stillness about him, your mother spoke of you in the present tense and your dear brother tried to distract me as much as possible even as he was grappling with life without you. The two of you were very close. I never realized how much he was affected by your departure. It takes a while to grow compassion for others when in the depths of grief.

I returned to Spring semester classes and gradually started to get back into the daily activities of life. My parents were watching me carefully and were feeling encouraged that I was getting back to normal, whatever that was. I gave them what they wanted, but I felt so anxious and unfocused. I was an empty container going through the motions. The light inside me was barely lit

What I needed was someone to talk to that would understand what I was going through. We communicated on so many things together. Now I was on my own. Friends and family were supportive, but were cautious around me. Few wanted to be reminded of the remnants of a war that was so unpopular and counseling was hardly available back then, even for the returning veterans.

The common thought was that I was young and resilient and

would rebound over time. I wanted to believe them. I was so broken, that I lost confidence in my own beliefs. Everything was up for question.

There were times when I felt that I could not catch my breath. I was sent to the family physician who at that time diagnosed it as hyperventilation caused by stress. He accompanied that with a prescription for Valium. That served as a sufficient mask for a while. I heard the sighs of relief all around me.

Valium was a temporary antidote. They were magic pills that could deaden the pain, shorten the day and elongate sleep. A perfect solution, but I knew deep down that I was attempting to banish feelings that would eventually have their day.

I had an indication that the pot was ready to boil over. One summer day, about three months after the funeral, I rolled down the windows, accelerated the engine and attempted to drive straight into a concrete wall. Something stopped me short of a few feet from the wall. I pulled over and sobbed until the tears poured out and I came to my senses. I went home and flushed the pills down the toilet. I had to find another way to deal with the pain.

Two things saved me: running and writing. The combination was my therapy. Still, today, when I am overwhelmed I pick up the pen or put on my sneakers (these days, to walk, not run). They are my faithful companions on the road of life. They never fail me.

Questions continued to roam around in my head. Who would hold my hand or sneak a kiss? Who would I comfort when there was a frightening situation? Who would I fall asleep and wake up with? With whom would I have a family? Who would I laugh with at a ridiculous situation? Whose heart would beat next to mine when we danced? Who would call me "babe" and I would be OK with it? Who would I be without you?

I had to recreate my life, piece by piece. I gingerly moved forward, but I always knew that you would never be fully gone from my heart, even though the material memories were securely placed in that suitcase. Your earthly journey ended and mine was taking me on another path. I had to learn to live without you, one step at a time.

A few years after the Washington D.C. Vietnam Memorial was completed I went there and touched your name on that national monument. I felt satisfied that you and all the others were acknowledged for your place in history. Even though there were large crowds, few words were spoken. It had the solemnity of a gravesite. The size and magnitude of this remembrance wall had a potent effect on every visitor, regardless of age or background.

I had a similar experience when I visited the 9/11 Memorial in New York City. It was the first time I returned to that site since 2003, when my job in the city ended. The memories of that day flooded back through the multitude of sensory exhibits. The visitors there were also respective and pensive.

The visual cues reminded me of our universal fragility and strength. Every human, no matter what side of the planet we reside, has struggles, tragedies and obstacles to overcome. Death may be the great equalizer; yet the human spirit somehow spurs us on to move ahead, even when we are dragging our proverbial feet.

When I visited both sites, I was reminded that I am not alone in this dance of life and that by looking back it is possible to rebuild and restore a soul.

You thoroughly squeezed a lot of life out of barely 20 years. You were not afraid of death. I didn't realize it at the time that you would have a continuous presence within the deepest part of me. I had so much more to learn in the years to come and that I would, once again, find comfort wrapped in our eternal love.

Yours forever,
Me

"Promise me you'll always remember: You're braver than you believe, and stronger than you seem, and smarter than you think."
~A. A. Milne

THE CONVERSATION

I have always maintained a healthy skepticism regarding the world of psychic phenomena. I definitely relate to the spiritual and mystical world, but I've never taken psychic readings seriously.

Although I've indulged in a few readings over the years, with two exceptions, they were mostly just amusing and general in nature, done for fun, rather than for any serious future advice and most things never came to fruition. Before this occurrence, I certainly had no interest in encountering anyone from the past. I figured let the past stay in the past.

When I recounted this particular experience to a trusted source, she suggested that I reach out to a highly skilled medium that did a lot of work with the grieving. I was advised she probably wouldn't be able to contact me for months, maybe not till the end of the following year.

I wasn't in any rush. I was still reading through the letters and living in a parallel universe between the past and present, struggling to make sense out of everything that was happening. I didn't expect much to come out of it. Would I even have contact with Chip after 50 years? Chances were slim.

After doing some research on Lynn and how mediums

functioned, I made the call and left a message, indicating the referral, not expecting to hear back for a long time. The answering message did confirm that appointments probably wouldn't be made before a lengthy period of time. I quickly forgot about it.

A few weeks later the phone rang and it was Lynn telling me she had a cancellation and asked if I would like the appointment later in the week. Her voice was full of joy and enthusiasm. It was like speaking to an old friend. As a career consultant I know when someone enjoys what they do.

I was surprised by the quick turn in events, but given everything that had recently occurred, anything that seemed strange before was now starting to feel normal. She advised me to record the session on my phone so I would have reference to it later because there would be a lot covered. This is the conversation pertaining to Chip that transpired.

SESSION WITH LYNN LECLERE – 11/6/20

LYNN: There's a man with your dad who is like a son to him. He's here with him. Your dad is standing right next to him. He wants you to know that he is with him. He keeps on giving so much love to you.
LYNN: Anything with a middle name starting in J? He is saying, middle name starts with a J. Does that make sense to you?
BARBARA: Yes, my middle name starts with a J.
LYNN: Wait a minute; I have to calm him down. He is so excited. He's kissing you. Tell her I'm so sorry. You are not alone. He has not left you alone. He says that it bothers him when you say he left you. Understand? He gets very upset. He gets upset when you are upset. He's here with you. I haven't left you, he keeps saying.
LYNN: He's talking about the book. Does that make sense? You don't have to tell me.

BARBARA: Yes. Should I write the book?
LYNN: Tell the story, he says.
LYNN: Give me a second. I have to calm him down again. He's saying a lot of things. He keeps telling me you were the blessing in his life. He says he must have done something good in his life that God blessed him with you.
BARBARA: Did he suffer when he died?
LYNN: Let me ask him.
LYNN: No. He's showing me a hard time breathing and touching his stomach area. He's also talking about a very difficult time breathing and he's making me feel like his heart is pounding. He's also makes me feel anxious or anxiety.
BARBARA: As he was dying?
LYNN: Yes.
BARBARA: Of course, it was a helicopter crash.
LYNN: Oh, My God!
BARBARA: I feel him all around me.
LYNN: He is around you. He died young. I feel anxiety. Not enough oxygen around his face. He can't breathe and something happened to his stomach, this poor guy.
BARBARA: What was his last thought? Was he thinking of me?
LYNN: I always thought of her, he says. You were always in his thoughts, mind and prayers, he's telling me. He felt he was the luckiest guy with you.
BARBARA: I just read that in his letter last night.
BARBARA: I'll always love him. Is it ok for me to love again? Is that what he wants? Is that the reason for rediscovering the letters?
LYNN: Absolutely!
BARBARA: It's so hard to have this beautiful first love. Everything else was like settling. I don't want to do that anymore.
LYNN: Did he have an Irish/German looking mother? She absolutely loved you and never stopped loving you.
BARBARA: Yes. She treated me like a daughter.

BARBARA: Does he want me to reach out to his brother?
LYNN: He would love that, he just said.
BARBARA: We had our whole life planned together and it went up in smoke with that explosion.
LYNN: He says you put your life on hold and you lived your life for everyone else but your own life.
BARBARA: I'm starting to live my life for me.
LYNN: He's so happy about that. He's so happy to be part of it, he's telling me.
BARBARA: When I die will Chip be there for me?
LYNN: Oh my God, he just said, yes!
LYNN: Who is Robert or Bob?
BARBARA: Robert is the man who is a fireman like he was and who brought me to the firehouse about six weeks ago to see his memorial plaque. I had all of his letters hidden in a suitcase with all of our memories. After 50 years, I opened the suitcase with the letters he wrote to me. That day brought me right back to then. I love him as much as I did 50 years ago. It's an extraordinary experience, feeling this all again. As I'm reading the letters, I'm writing him back in today's time. I feel him so close to me. I never knew if there was anyone there on the other side.
LYNN: That's what's going to be the book, he's telling me. Tell it through the letters that love doesn't die. He loves you with all of his heart, he's telling me and he's never stopped loving you. He's never stopped watching over you.
BARBARA: Will I be able to love in that way again?
LYNN: He's telling me, yes, but it's a different love. He's telling me you were his first love. When you have that first love there's nothing in the world that compares to that first love. You understand? There are some people who don't get to go through life with that first person, but they never stop loving their first love. He's explaining that you're his first love. Nothing in the world compares to it. Nothing compares when your heart is so pure and open and

so innocent. He says, it's the true essence of the innocence of love. Because the heart never got hurt, it's in its pureness. And then, life happens and hurts come into the heart. Do you understand?
BARBARA: Yes. I always felt like I had this black cloud over me with relationships after him. Relationships turned to dust. They just weren't right.
LYNN: He's emphasizing that it's never going to be that pureness of what you had. He wants you to have love and he'll be the first one to greet you on the other side and love you and have time with you on the other side. He does want you to experience love here.
LYNN: He's telling me opening up the letters, opened up your heart again. That was the purpose of opening the letters again, to open up your heart to the idea of love again. The heart can love many at the same time. Your love is getting full again. He's excited for you, he's telling me. This feels like decades of your heart shut down.
BARBARA: I've have a hard time trusting again since he died.
LYNN: He's telling me you are learning to love and to trust. This is the perfect time. He gets such a kick out of you. The intimacy and vulnerability will take time.
LYNN: He says you were so restricted being brought up. This is now like being free.
BARBARA: By reading the letters he wrote to me and I to him, I realize how much I meant to him and my capacity for love and It's been bottled up. I'm learning to appreciate my life. I'm falling back in love with him and myself and maybe I'll fall in love again, too.
LYNN: You're opening up your heart again, he's telling me. He'll never stop loving you, he says. He's telling me he absolutely adores you.
LYNN: You are still integrating this experience. He is so excited for you. It's like going to the next level and you have to integrate it.

BARBARA: It's like climbing a mountain. You have to stop on each plateau before moving ahead.
BARBARA: Did he orchestrate all of this?
LYNN: Absolutely! It was perfect timing. Everything is perfect timing, he says. He wants you to know everything is in perfect Divine timing. He wants you to know that.
LYNN: What was happening in September & October?
BARBARA: This experience started in September. That's when I reopened his letters.
LYNN: Is it an old fashioned stiff suitcase, like a box? That's what he's showing me. There's a jewel or jewelry in there.
BARBARA: There's all of our memorabilia, pressed flowers and a ring. That's where our history is chronicled. His writing is so beautiful.
LYNN: He keeps showing me Jimmy Stewart in "It's a Wonderful Life." I don't know why he's showing me it.
BARBARA: Maybe it's about believing in angels?
LYNN: He just wanted to see the world with you.
BARBARA: I've been seeing the world. Maybe he's been with me in my travels.
LYNN: He loves traveling and to see so many different things.
BARBARA: We both liked the same things, like two peas in a pod. We wanted to travel so much. Even in Vietnam he saw some part of it as an adventure. He was exhilarated and scared at the same time, especially when he did a good job and no one was hurt or killed. He was responsible, smart and in school to be an engineer. He was preparing to finish college when he came back. The war made no sense to me. But he went with it. What got him through the difficult times was writing to me and I understand that because by writing to him now, I feel so relieved.
BARBARA: Does he know I am writing him letters?
LYNN: Absolutely!
LYNN: He says he's never stopped thinking of you. What got him through the days was thinking of you. The happiest day was

when he was going to be reunited with you. He planned a whole life with you through the letters.

BARBARA: When he died and he realized our life was severed, what happened?

LYNN: He still watched over his parents, his brother and he always watched over you. He's always watched out over you.

BARBARA: Was he sad that he didn't get to live this life here with me?

LYNN: Absolutely. He's says he's not worried about it, though, because he will share his life with you. He knows that there is no doubt about it and that is what is precious. He waits for you, but he wants you to experience the physical love down here. Do you understand? It's like you weren't ready for love again and now you are.

BARBARA: He's freed me up through these letters.

LYNN: He's excited that you are free to love again. You are still so young. There is still so much living to do.

LYNN: He keeps on talking about Italy. He loved Italy with you. He was there with you and loved it. It was like his dreams. Absolutely beautiful!

LYNN: He's talking about Tuscany. It's beautiful and scenic, breathtakingly beautiful like you, he says he shared it with you. He wants you to know he was there with you.

BARBARA: Ask him about the cat burglars who stole my stuff.

LYNNE: He said he couldn't have control over it, but, you learned.

LYNN: He's talking about your garden. He loves you in the garden. He goes to the garden with you. He wants you to know that.

LYNN: He's giving me Christmas.

BARBARA: We met the first Friday in December before Christmas. Our first Christmas together was magical.

LYNN: Your first Christmas was the most special thing in his heart. He treasured that.

BARBARA: It's still my favorite holiday. Tell him I'll put a gift under the tree for him this year.
LYNN: He said, tell her no. She is my gift. That is so cute!
LYNN: He put a sticker on the suitcase.
BARBARA: I don't know what that's about.
LYNN: Anything about teaching or counseling?
BARBARA: That's what I do in my work.
LYNN: That's beautiful, he says. He loves that you do that.
LYNN: One thing: He wants you to stop being so hard on yourself. That's very important.
Barbara: OK
LYNN: Oh, he is the most romantic guy! Holy, good god! He's is an old soul. They don't make them like this.
BARBARA: This is why it's so hard. This was" knock your socks off" love. It felt like we picked up where we left off before. That's how it felt when we met.
LYNN: He absolutely adores you.
BARBARA: That explosion ripped me apart when it ripped him apart.
LYNN: He feels the same way.
LYNN: He misses his brother also. One of his nephews is named after him and it made him so happy and he's so proud. He loves the boys. He loves his brother. You were always part of the family. They loved you and still love you.
BARBARA: His mom told me I was the daughter they didn't have and always considered me part of the family. I loved them very much. Over the years, I would see his mother and one time she told me that she and his father hoped we had eloped before he went to Vietnam so it would have been official. I always felt safe with them.
LYNN: They still love you up here.
BARBARA: I wanted to have his last name. It felt so right.
LYNN: It was right.
LYNN: He's telling me Brooklyn. It must be his dad. I'm feeling his dad.

BARBARA: He may have been born there.
LYNN: His parents met when they were young. They came from different religions.
BARBARA: I don't remember that.
LYNN: He loves you. There's a picture of you that you kiss of his.
BARBARA: It's right near me.
LYNN: When you kiss it, his heart goes pitter patter. He loves that. He says, mother gave the picture to you. You must have gotten picture from his mother.
BARBARA: I'm not sure.
LYNN: He has his dog with him. Oh my god, does he loves this dog!
BARBARA: Yes, Smoky. Did he send my dog to me?
LYNN: He's laughing. Your dog is smaller; his is bigger. He says your dog doesn't like it when he comes in to visit. He starts growling and gets up and goes to another place.
BARBARA: I hadn't noticed that.
LYNN: His God given name is Lester.
BARBARA: He was named after his father; a chip off the old block.
LYNN: He says, she's so brave. You don't give yourself enough credit. You are a lot stronger than you give yourself credit for and very smart.
LYNN: He's blowing kisses at you with both hands. It's the cutest thing. He says, this was the best time with you. He loved sharing this time with you.
BARBARA: He drew pictures of him doing that in his letters.
LYNN: That's going to make an amazing book. You have to write the book!
BARBARA: I will. Thank you.
LYNN: You take good care of yourself. All blessings to you.

. . .

When the phone call ended, I said out loud to an empty room, "what just happened?" I felt as if a jolt of lightning had just gone through me. Emotions were firing within me during the session and after it. Everything that was spoken was accurate and no one could possibly have known this information, if it hadn't come from the "other side."

It was too big to wrap my arms around. I had to listen to the recording several times over the next few days to digest all that was said and affirm that I hadn't been dreaming. My instincts told me this would somehow transform me but I wouldn't know the extent of it for several months. It was a gradual process.

It took me a few weeks to reach out to his brother. It had been so many years since we spoke and I was a bit anxious to initiate the call. How would he respond to such a story? Would he believe me? Would it open up old wounds? Every time I had a question, I went back to the conversation and followed Chip's words.

When I made the call, we picked up where we left off. We both agreed that it was tough to take this all in but he believed me. He revealed how Chip's death changed him as much as it changed me. He has also felt his presence at times in his life. We are the only two left who could share our experience of knowing him in such an intimate manner. It was so comforting to talk about the things we couldn't speak about 50 years ago. He also served as my memory for the details I had forgotten over the years.

He verified the information about his parents, his son's name, and the military information provided surrounding Chip's death which he had continued to research over the subsequent years.

I thanked him for being there for me during that difficult time. I now know he put aside his own feelings to be supportive to me and his family. It isn't easy being the survivor of a sibling's death particularly under such difficult circumstances. We had to handle our grief in our own quiet manner unaccompanied with the labels of parent or wife.

I look forward to seeing him and meeting his family. There's a part of Chip living on in them. Like everything else that has happened, Chip has worked his magic in bringing us back together again.

It had been a long time since I watched "It's a Wonderful Life". This time I saw it from a different perspective. I think he wanted me to know that I matter, my life has purpose and I am exactly where I'm supposed to be. It's as if he has a much broader view and wants me to zero in on the important things. His physical being may be gone, but he hasn't lost his insight, sense of humor and desire to champion my well being.

The only loose end was the sticker on the suitcase. About a week after the session, I was going through some art supplies and a sticker fell out of a package. It says, "This Happened." It is now firmly adhered to the suitcase close to the handle. I think it's a reminder that if at any time I question if this is all real, it serves as an affirmation that it absolutely did happen. I believe he's chuckling and having a good time making me laugh at the magical absurdity of this encounter.

Recently, I reached out to Lynn and talked with her about the book I was writing. I asked her how she felt about including the transcribed session and without hesitation she said "Absolutely! You have my permission. It's yours to do as you wish." She also said "it would be her pleasure to be part of this amazing story." Again, the spirits aligned to make this endeavor a reality. I am grateful for her magnanimous support.

"Somebody should tell us, right at the start of our lives that we are dying. Then we might live life to the limit. Do it! I say, whatever you want to do, do it now! There are only so many tomorrows."
~Michael Landon

REFLECTIONS

It is almost shocking when half of an equation doesn't stop existing when the other half dies. We are never prepared for death, even when you watch someone withering away and know what is coming. We know it exists. We all have to experience it and, in some ways, it may appear as a welcoming relief when life gets too hard, but ultimately it is not like the preparation for a trip. It's permanent. No return ticket. It is more about unpacking, sifting through the essentials and then letting go.

As a solo experience, its mystery is larger than life and we cannot stop it, not for ourselves or for another. It's completely out of our control. I think we fear that lack of control more than the process itself. It can shake our belief system to its core. It can also make us more observant, empathic and compassionate.

And, what about the ones left behind? It's our job to pick up the pieces and move forward. Love can't stop death, but we can be transformed by it. That is the biggest gift I received from opening that suitcase. That suitcase held a treasure chest of knowledge that I have just begun to understand and incorporate into my life. After all the resurrected pain, it was entirely worth it. I am forever changed by this experience. I would not be the person I'm becoming without it. No matter what happens, our love will always be a part of me.

That's why I like the term "collateral beauty." It means that out of difficulty and even tragedy we can find the silver lining in the love that continues to exist. The trauma not only brings us closer to the mystery of death, it helps us to live more fully, appreciating the continuity of life. It reminds us that we are more than our physical bodies and that by giving and receiving love, we can accept where the darkness takes us and find joy in the ultimate light of being. When we know that we are truly loved, everything changes, no matter the source.

I have learned to deal with fear by doing the thing that scares me. I take that cue from Eleanor Roosevelt: "*do one thing every day that scares you.*" Even though flying came naturally to me, the idea of getting on a helicopter terrified me. I could never get that vision of the explosion out of my head. However, on a trip to Alaska, I allowed my excitement to experience being in a helicopter landing on an iceberg to overcome my fear. My heart pounded loudly all the way there and back, but in between, on that iceberg, with the wonder of its deep blue crevices, I experienced the most divine peace.

When my corporate work demanded I make presentations in front of large and small groups of people, I got involved in community theatre to overcome my stage fright. Being in another character helped, but before delivering my first lines, I was sweating through my costumes at times. But, I learned to trust myself by inhabiting the characters and knowing that I wouldn't let the cast or audience down.

As I chipped away at fearful situations, stumbling along the way at times with great anxiety, I've regained a modicum of confidence in my ability to handle the tough stuff.

I've spent the last days and hours with several people who were dear to me before they passed over. They were some of the most beautiful and enlightening moments of my life, honored to experience death up so close with souls who taught me how to live, make every moment count and complete this life with a fulfilling passage. They are my greatest teachers.

What I witnessed is that it can be a fearless, peaceful, even joyful experience if we choose it that way. My friend, Jim told me before he passed that he taught others to stay in the present but he never realized how significant the present was till he struggled with his final breaths. I learned to say "thank you" every morning as my first words, for the incredible gift of each breath.

No matter how many books I've read, workshops I've attended or discussions I've encountered, most of life remains a mystery. Seeking happiness has been a waste of my time. Staying curious has served me. Curiosities about nature, space, time, history, culture, human actions astound me, mostly in a good way.

Taking a cue from Chip, let me find things out for myself, rather than borrowing other's opinions. He is residing in another side of life and I have my life here to further explore. The funny thing is that the more I explore, the more I realize how little I know. And, that keeps me humble, and also thirsty for new adventure.

Lynn's session opened me up to the belief of life beyond death. I now have been straddling two worlds and still assimilating its meaning. When I stand outside of myself and view this as someone's else's story and I witness the day in the hair salon, the visit to the firehouse memorial, the suitcase of letters, the timely session with Lynne and the decision to tell this story, it's quite extraordinary yet plausible. It's an invitation to open up my heart, listen attentively to my inner voice, and take a deep dive into the impossible. Some of the shackles I've held close to me are falling away.

The letters reminded me of the power of love. No matter how much time has passed between us, it still exists. It's as potent today as it was 50 years ago. It is just geography separating us. Love is its own master.

My niece and nephew are to be married in the next two years. I wish for them and their respective spouses to have the happiness I've experienced, to not take anything for granted and to keep loving even when it's hard to do.

As I return the letters to the suitcase, this time it is with different feelings. It is no longer to shut out the past and suffocate the emotions, but to smile with a grateful heart for the memory of loving and being loved so completely and that he has always been with me all these years. He gave me back the pieces missing in me. The treasure is now inside of me to own and take on my journey.

I recall the movie, Titanic, when at the end Rose went on to have a fulfilling life, but, held on to the diamond pendant as a reminder of those few poignant days that changed her life. She joyfully sent it into the ocean and she was free to move ahead, presumably to meet Jack again. She went back to go forward. I certainly get that now.

I want to leave the tank empty, thoroughly used up by life experiences, before I leave this earthly plane. I don't know where the next bend in the road will take me. I can only trust life, with its twists and turns, to show me the way. I may stumble and fall, make mistakes and not always do the right thing. But, I know I can overcome those things with a grateful heart.

I hope to fulfill Chip's wish for me; to love again, not in the same way, but just as lovely. I like to think that person will have those good qualities he had, and that I trust him to be beside me as I make my passage and willingly release me to take Chip's hand on the "other side" fulfilling Chip's last request to have that dance he owes me. In the meantime, I will be looking up at the stars and smiling, thinking of Meister Eckhart's words, "*trust in the magic of new beginnings.*"

"Your pain is the breaking of the shell that encloses your understanding."
~Kahlil Gibran

AUTHOR'S NOTE

My life has been transformed through this process. It started by saying "yes" to a stranger and showing up. Upon reflection I've learned the following:

PAY ATTENTION TO DETAILS

From the day we are born and put our tiny fist in our mouth our lives are made up of a continuous string of details. In the course of a day we have experienced over a million of them either washing dishes, brushing our teeth, walking the dog, doing our job or lending an ear to another human being in need of talking through something.

Our lives are rich with moments that we can't possibly remember. Yet, we do savor those details, particularly, when we look back on our lives and remember the shared experiences with others. There is a reciprocity of bearing witness to our existence that allows us to live on in the minds and hearts of others.

TIME IS A CONCEPT

That's a hard one to grasp. Most of our lives are dictated by the clock. We are scheduled and sometimes over-scheduled beings, who are programmed to believe that everything that happens is within the confines of time. But, if we enlarge our thoughts about time and gaze at the stars or indulge in the vastness of the universe, we are directly confronted with the contradiction to our concept of time. There's a world beyond us that we may not understand or even embrace, but even with our skepticism, stay open to the possibility.

Yes, we have to get things done within a segment of time but we can live in a much broader view of what life is and what becomes of us after we leave our mortal beings. This doesn't have to originate from a religious or philosophical belief. Just look at nature to expand our vision. A tree doesn't count its rings to tell its age; we do that. We minimize the tree's greatness by giving it a timeline and we diminish our ability to see our true identity beyond birth and death

EMBRACE GRIEF

Grief is a great teacher. We can set it aside or lock it in a suitcase, but it's always there. We just put a cover on it. It wants to be heard. There are the small griefs such as not getting that shiny red bicycle we wanted, burying our pet frog or losing a job. The big griefs are the ones that come from out of nowhere and slay us, causing us to lose our breath, break our heart or our mind.

Grief has its own timeline. There are plenty of books about how long the grief process should take with benchmarks in the road. What I realized that every person's grief process is different. Mine was contained for decades until its present emergence. At times, we may think we are over the hump and then we are back on the sadness highway. Be kind to yourself and let it show you the way.

When we have the courage to break open and let the grief pore out we become lighter, more compassionate beings. It's painful and turbulent, but ultimately, if we stay the course we can come upon our greatest realization, that we are stronger, braver and more resilient than we believe ourselves to be.

SAY YES TO LIFE

Don't allow fear to overcome joy. Fear has been my companion for most of my life. Yet, when I've pushed through it or smacked it aside, I've had the most incredible experiences. Get comfortable with being uncomfortable. If you are afraid to fly, do it anyway. The destination will provide amazing memories that will far outweigh the discomfort of flying. Anyway, there are pills for that.

Don't leave the earth with regrets no matter how short or long our lifespan. Leave graciously with a light heart. Death is a common denominator We never know when that day arrives when we must depart, but we all will experience it.

Take a walk in a graveyard. The departed all had our worries, pains and grievances along with the gains, celebrations and joyful moments. They can teach us about the choices we can make on how to live our lives. We have that power, even on the days when we feel weak and frightened. Don't wait till you are close to your last days to truly live. Do it now!

REMEMBER THE MILITARY

Those women and men are our protectors. They put their lives on the line during war and peaceful times. Every time a person in military service steps into their role, whether on the ground, air, vessel or behind the scene, there are a host of people behind them who care and whose lives are changed by their work. Consider their sacrifices.

You don't have to be a flag waver or even believe in the conflict. Just support what they are doing. They may be being doing a job that allows us to sit comfortably at home, eating dinner and watching Netflix.

LEAVE SOMETHING BEHIND

Write something, anything besides a text or a tweet. Show someone that they matter. Allow them the indulgence of opening a card or a letter with a sentiment you wrote with heartfelt words. Don't be afraid to express in writing what is sometimes difficult to say in person. Think of the recipient saving it in a box or draw and opening it on a grey day when they need to know they matter.

Texts and tweets have a shelf life and are easily discarded. Written words keep the memories alive. They leave a universal legacy for others to know that they are not alone. They tell something about a life lived. Letters brought me back to life. Imagine what your words can do for someone you care about.

ACKNOWLEDGMENTS

This book wouldn't have been possible without the precious people in my circle that supported me through this process and the ebb and flow of life. Profound gratitude to my champions, Lhea Scotto for sharing her wisdom, generous direction and belief in this story; to Regina Feeney, consummate researcher, archivist and friend who always says "you've got this!"; to Carlo Mignano for friendship and creative partnerships and to Janet Cuneo for literally and figuratively walking this path with me every step of the way.

I am immensely grateful to Stephanie Larkin and the amazing staff at Red Penguin. Thank you for believing in this story and launching it out into the universe.

Special thanks to Anne Kane, my guardian angel; to Donna Cariello, Hope ambassador who makes the world a better place; Rony Kessler for sharing your experience and your patience answering all of my questions; Nancy Aronie for honoring the writer and showing me that our words are sacred gifts; Tony Bellizzi who not only gives hope to the children but also gives us the creative space to share our musings and Lynn Leclere who made the intangible, tangible and opened me to the world beyond.

To the Lakeview Fire Department for honoring their brother, especially Robert Hockenjos for being the catalyst and George Motschmann who created the vision for the commemoration.

Big hugs to my dear friends who enrich my life in so many

ways and to my goddess and retreat sisters. I am so grateful we are part of each other's history. The years together have given me strength, comfort and an abundance of joyous memories. You make all the pieces fit!

To the FML memoir group which continues to inspire me with your courage and extraordinary life stories.

To Paul, my memory, sharing our love for your brother and for being there for me when I couldn't be there for myself.

To my family who is always close in my heart even when geography gets in the way. Your love is a gift I don't take for granted.

Finally, to my beloved co-author. Young hearts are tender. You held mine gently and firmly for which I am forever grateful. Thank you for the gift of eternal love and the reminder that our bodies may crumble and turn to dust, but words are immortal. All roads lead me back to you.

ABOUT THE AUTHOR

Barbara J. Spinelli is a former finance industry leader, now a career consultant assisting people in finding and fortifying their career path. She is also the co-chairperson of a community business center supporting the development and growth of new and existing small businesses. She holds a B.A. from Adelphi University and a Master's degree in Organizational Counseling from New York Institute of Technology.

Barbara has always balanced her professional life with her creative enterprises. As a prolific published poet, she has hosted numerous poetry events in a variety of settings. She has also collaborated on documentaries supporting children's causes and hosts a regular memoir group since 2014, producing anthologies showcasing the member's works.

Barbara also is a successful mixed media artist who has had her works exhibited in several venues and had a one-woman show sponsored by the Long Island Artists Council of Freeport, NY.

PHOTOS

Young Chip on the right with brother, Paul and father, Lester, Sr.

Chip's Fireman's Installation with author

Camera Shy - fun times soon after we met

Boot Camp, Ft. Jackson, SC

In the field, Vietnam

Swimming in a bomb crater, a day at the beach!, Vietnam

Tay Ninh Base, Vietnam

River boat patrolling, Vietnam

Bob, the Fire Commissioner who brought author to see the commemorative plaque

Suitcase filled with letters

READING GROUP GUIDE

1. The author states that grief has no timeline. Do you agree? Have you had a situation in which you put your grief aside, only to have it show up later in your life? What has it taught you about the grieving process?

2. Several events throughout the story indicate a synchronicity of people showing up to assist in the writer's process. When have events fallen into place that make you realize that something greater may be involved in your destiny? Where you aware of it at the time or does it occur to you through retrospection?

3. During the medium's dialogue, it is said that first love is pure and undamaged by life's ups and downs. Have you experienced love in this manner? What has it taught you about relationships? Can the purity of love be sustained? Has your first love continued to be a positive experience in your life?

4. The letters have a powerful and lasting impact on the writer's life. Have you received something in writing that changed your thoughts or feelings about a situation? What did you realize

about yourself and the other person? Have you kept the written memory? What impact have written words had on your life?

5. The writer has conflict between loving the soldier and hating the war. Have you ever been conflicted in a similar manner? How comfortable are you in between the two powerful emotions? Do you think it is a viable notion to straddle both sides of the issues?

6. The author's beliefs were changed regarding life after death. Have you always believed there is more after departing? If not, what changed your mind? What experience have you encountered to create more certainty about life after death? Has it alleviated a fear of dying?

7. Physical and emotional pain is a topic that runs through the book. Which is more difficult to handle? Chip feels the physical pain during training and the emotional pain by being separated from his love. Do you think he balances it well in his letters? Has writing ever relieved your emotional pain? If not, what does?

8. Through the letters, the author reflects not only on her life with Chip, but also on the experiences before and after him? Do you believe she has gained a clearer perspective with the passage of time? When have you looked back and discovered new things about yourself? Did they enlighten or frighten you? What did you do with the discoveries?

9. The letters occur in a context of a historical time and place evoking strong emotions after five decades. Do you think if the dates and locations were different, the story would resonate throughout time? Can the written word stand the test of time? If she opened the suitcase at another time in her life, would the story have a different meaning?

10. So much of the romance between them was around simple things (i.e. walk in the park, music, letters, snowstorm). Do you think romance is still alive in this age of technological communication? Does enjoyment with small gestures and experiences hold up today? Is it possible to create a more simple life to be happy?

11. The author uses the term "collateral beauty." She found restoration from this experience. Do you believe that there are silver linings from the harshest of situations? Can we create beauty from trauma? Can we find joy after loss?

www.ingramcontent.com/pod-product-compliance
Lightning Source LLC
Chambersburg PA
CBHW060606080526
44585CB00013B/709